LIFE AND TIMES OF ANN BAILEY

The Pioneer Heroine of the Great Kanawha Valley

by Virgil A. Lewis

ANN BAILEY.

CABIN OF ANN BAILEY.

It was on the Ohio River Hills, below Gallipolis,
and built by her of fence rails.

LIFE AND TIMES

—— OF ——

ANN BAILEY

THE PIONEER HEROINE

—— OF THE ——

GREAT KANAWHA VALLEY

—— BY ——

VIRGIL A. LEWIS

SECRETARY
West Virginia Historical and Antiquarian Society.

*Corresponding Member of the Virginia Historical Society;
Member Pennsylvania Historical Society; Corresponding Member of the
Western Reserve Historical Society of Cleveland;
and Author of the* History of West Virginia.

"Out of monuments, names, wordes, proverbs, traditions,
private records, fragments of stories, passages of bookes and the like,
we doe save and recover somewhat from the deluge of time."
— *Bacon.*

Mark S. Phillips Publishing
Proctorville, Ohio
MCMXCVIII

Part I previously published in 1891 as
Life and Times of Anne Bailey, The Pioneer Heroine of the Great Kanawha Valley
by The Butler Printing Company of Charleston, West Virginia.

Part II previously published in 1907.

Both books are complete and unabridged.
In Part I, the spelling of Ann Bailey's name has been corrected (dropping
the "e" from Anne) to bring it to the form generally accepted today.
All other spellings, of both words and proper names, have not been changed
in order to keep the proper flavor of the time period in which the book
was written. Obvious minor errors made in the original typography
(such as running words together without a space) have been corrected.

Library of Congress Catalog Card Number: 98-88393
ISBN: 0-9667246-0-7

Second Edition, Second Printing

Printed in Canada

mark s. phillips

p u b l i s h i n g

Proctorville, Ohio

www.marksphillips.com

TABLE OF CONTENTS

PART I
Life and Times of Ann Bailey

PREFACE ix

CHAPTER I 1
THE HERO WOMEN OF THE WEST.

CHAPTER II 5
THE PLACE AND DATE OF ANN BAILEY'S BIRTH.

CHAPTER III 9
ANN BAILEY'S MARRIAGE AND RESIDENCE IN THE COLONY
OF VIRGINIA.

CHAPTER IV 13
THE AUGUSTA HOME AND THE BATTLE OF POINT PLEASANT
– DEATH OF RICHARD TROTTER.

CHAPTER V 17
A REMARKABLE CAREER OF FEMALE HEROISM – ELEVEN
YEARS OF WIDOWHOOD – HER SECOND MARRIAGE.

CHAPTER VI 21
REMOVAL TO CLENDENIN'S FORT – MILITARY AFFAIRS IN THE
KANAWHA VALLEY.

CHAPTER VII 25
SCENE AT FORT CHARLESTON – ANN BAILEY'S RIDE – SHE
SAVES THE GARRISON FROM MASSACRE – HER SECOND
WIDOWHOOD.

CHAPTER VIII 37
THE PEOPLE AMONG WHOM ANN BAILEY LIVED.

CHAPTER IX 45
REMINISCENCES OF ANN BAILEY – HER TWENTY-SEVEN
YEARS' RESIDENCE IN THE KANAWHA VALLEY.

CHAPTER X 51
LAST VISIT TO CHARLESTON – HER SON WILLIAM – REMOVAL
NORTH OF THE OHIO RIVER.

CHAPTER XI 55
THE REMOVAL AND RESIDENCE NORTH OF THE OHIO RIVER –
ANN BAILEY'S CABIN – HER DEATH AND BURIAL – HER
DESCENDENTS.

PART II

Ann Bailey: Thrilling Adventures of the Heroine of the Kanawha Valley

ANN BAILEY Virgil A. Lewis 63

ANN BAILEY Mrs. Lillian Rozell Messenger 67

PART III
Additional Material

AFTERWORD Mark S. Phillips, Publisher 75

MAP & PHOTOGRAPHS 77

INDEX.. 82

ABOUT THE AUTHOR 85

ACKNOWLEDGMENTS & NOTES 86

PART I

LIFE AND TIMES OF ANN BAILEY

The Pioneer Heroine of the Great Kanawha Valley

by Virgil A. Lewis

(Previously Published in 1891)

PREFACE.

Is it possible at this late date to save from oblivion the Pioneer History of West Virginia? What shall the answer to this question be? That much of that history is now lost — gone with those who were the principal actors in the drama — is certain, but that very much yet remains and with proper effort, may be preserved from the ruthless hand of oblivion, is equally certain.

Our history is not so nearly lost as we are by some led to believe, and if this be true, then what is the chief source from which it can be preserved? I answer, from persons yet alive. In every county in the state there are many persons now living at the age of from sixty to eighty years old who were themselves acquainted with the actors in the border scenes when they were of like age. This carries us backward an hundred and twenty years, to the year 1770, so that for one hundred years at least, we may have a narrative of events, coming to us from creditable witnesses yet living, who learned the facts to which they testify, from those who were themselves the actors and witnesses of the scenes of which they have transmitted oral accounts. This is competent testimony, such as would be received in evidence in any court in the state.

Will our history be preserved? Judging from the present activity on all hands, and the increasing inquiry relative to the local and family history of our people now heard on every hand, the answer to this question must be an affirmative one. To-day in many counties of the state, local historians are busy collecting the traditions and reminiscences of their localities; the press of the state is devoting attention to this and kindred subjects, and state officials are for the first time collecting and putting in durable form the reports and public documents of the several departments, while books are rapidly multiplying in the state. Foremost in the task of collecting and preserving stands the West Virginia Historical and Antiquarian Society, an organization which is bending every energy to the work before it; and with the forces now employed, we predict that soon all of the past now possible to save from the ruthless hand of time will be gathered in its archives. But the work must be prosecuted rapidly. Time is passing hastily by and laying its blighting hand upon material things and with such destroying effects, that there remains not a year for suspended action. "Now or never" must be the watch-word of our people if they would preserve their own history and transmit it to those who are to come after them.

The following pages compose a mite of the work to be accomplished and no apology is therefore deemed necessary for its appearance.

V.A.L.

Charleston, W. Va.

CHAPTER I.

THE HERO WOMEN OF THE WEST.

The women who accompanied their husbands, brothers and sons in the march of civilization and the conquest of the wilderness were Spartans in all that the term implies. The embodiment of all that ennobles womankind, they possessed in a wonderful degree, a complete union of strength, courage, love, devotion, meekness and shrewdness which fitted them for the severe and often terrible ordeals through which they had to pass. Not only did they share the hardships and privations of frontier life, but they were familiar with war's dread alarm. From infancy to old age, from the cradle to the grave, their ears were saluted with the story of savage warfare, the reprisal, the ambuscade, the midnight burning, the stake, the scalping knife and the rencounters of rifle and tomahawk, were all familiar to them. But disregarding danger, toil and suffering and alone devoted to the safety of those composing their little households gathered in the cabin homes of the western border, these mothers and daughters nerved their arms and steeled their hearts to the severe duties that surrounded them. It was the Heroic Age of America and these the hero mothers of the Western Border and of the Revolution.

Other ages and other lands have produced women whose names are famous on the historic page. Indeed history is replete with examples of female heroism. Israel had her Deborah; Spain delights to dwell upon the memory of Isabella; while France glories in the names of her Joan of Arc and Lavellette. But two of these women unsexed themselves in the excitement of battle, one ingloriously stained her hands in human blood, and the other had nothing to lose by her successful efforts.

But the western heroines of our own land, without the *eclat* of female warriors, displayed more true courage throughout the long and stormy days of the Indian wars, and exhibited more of the true spirit of heroism, than any examples in ancient times or in modern history beyond our own land. The Greek matron who urged her son to the conflict charging him to return from the war with his shield, or see her face no more, displayed no higher degree of true courage, than did these Hero Women of the West. One of these has left her name indelibly impressed upon the pages of the history of the Great Kanawha Valley and the story of her life and adventures still lives in the traditions of the people. Several incidents relating to her, have been published, but no western chronicler has attempted to collect in connected narrative the story of Ann Bailey, the Pioneer Heroine of the Valley. In an attempt to do this, these pages have been written.

For generations in the traditional history of Ann Bailey has been transmitted from father to son and from mother to daughter, and to-day the traveler can scarcely stop at the home of an old family in the Great Kanawha Valley at which he could not hear some adventure recounted or anecdote related illustrative of the character of this remarkable woman.

But little relating to her has been written, and the major portion of that has been done since her death, and by persons who never saw her; hence, at this late day, we must rely almost entirely upon tradition for what may now be learned of her whose name for a century has been a household word in the valley of the Great Kanawha. But tradition, when accepted by common consent; when divested of everything of a mythical character, and when stripped of the fabulous, the imaginary and the fanciful, then, to the student as well as the writer of history, it becomes competent evidence and as such has been accepted in all ages of the world's history, as witness the following:

"Stand fast, hold the *traditions* which ye have been taught."
   2 Thess. ii. 15.

"Will you mock at an ancient *tradition* begun upon an
   honorable respect?" — *Shakespeare.*

"Naught but *tradition* remains of the beautiful village of
   Grand Pre." — *Longfellow.*

What is tradition? It may be defined as the unwritten delivery of
information concerning practices, customs and events transmitted
from father to son; from ancestors to descendants, or from one
generation to another, and in this sense, it is one of the pillars of
written history, and ceases to be tradition and becomes history when
it is written.

In the following pages everything not consistent with truth has
been eliminated and the accuracy of the work rests upon what has
been written in the past, relative to the subject, upon records and
upon the testimony of witnesses yet living who saw and conversed
with Ann Bailey. Among these are Colonel Charles B. Waggener, of
Point Pleasant, now in his eighty–fourth year; Mrs. Mary McCulloch,
of Mason County, now eighty–one years of age; Mrs. Mary Irions,
and Mrs. Phebe Willey, both of Gallia County, Ohio, the former in
her eighty–fourth year and the latter seventy–four years of age and
both grand–daughters of Ann Bailey; Mr. John Slack, Sr., of Charleston, now eighty–two years of age; and Mr. John H. Goshorn, also of
Charleston, now in the seventy–eighth year of his age.

CHAPTER II.

THE PLACE AND DATE
OF ANN BAILEY'S BIRTH.

That Ann Bailey, whose maiden name was Hennis, was born in England, and that the city of Liverpool was the place of her nativity, is established by an unbroken chain of testimony. She ever prided herself upon being born in England's western metropolis. But of the exact date of her birth, she was not herself certain, and it is safe to say that nothing connected with her history has been the subject of greater exaggeration than this; and for nearly three–quarters of a century, it has been the current belief and so stated by those who have written of her, that at the time of her death, she was a centenarian — and by some that she died in the one hundred and twenty-fifth year of her age.

Singular it is indeed that such an idea should have obtained when it was *almost* contrary to natural laws, when directly opposed to her own declaration, and when a little investigation would have set the matter right. Let us see what can be learned respecting the date:

Her father was a soldier in the wars with Queen Anne and served on the continent under the Duke of Marlborough, where with his regiment, he participated in the desperate battle of Blenheim. Returning to his home and family, he bestowed upon his infant daughter — the child of his old age — the name of *Ann* in honor of his beloved sovereign, whose banner he had so bravely defended in foreign lands.

In the year 1747, the mother, accompanied by the Queen's namesake, went from Liverpool to London to visit her brother; and there for the first time, and probably the last, the little daughter, as she well remembered, witnessed in her wonder and astonishment the splendors of the British capital.

It was while sojourning in London that an event occurred, which made such a lasting impression upon the child, and the scene then witnessed, wrought so much upon her mind, that all the years of her after life, could not efface it and she talked of it until the time of her death, ever asserting that she was then *five* years of age.

This even was the public execution of Lord Lovat, upon a charge of treason, and now if we can fix the date of that execution, from which she reckoned time, we can then readily arrive at the *date of her birth*. All English authorities agree as to the time.

Simon Frazer Lovat, was born about the year 1676, and was the second son of Thomas, afterwards the twelfth Lord Lovat. He took his degrees at King's College, Aberdeen, where he gained a good knowledge of the Latin Classics.

One of his first acts after leaving school was to organize a body of three hundred men, ostensibly, to be a part of a regiment in the service of William and Mary and in which he was to hold a commission; but his real purpose, as he afterwards avowed, was to have at his command a body of trained men whom he could, at any time, carry over to the interest of James.

His next act was to bring about a forced marriage with the widow of his elder brother by which he secured the title and estates of the deceased. But the family of Lady Lovat began a prosecution against him and he fled to the Highlands, and later sought refuge in France, where, by various intrigues, he soon gained favor at the court of Versailles.

From there he directed a secret military organization in the north of Scotland, which arose in the interest of the Pretender in the rebellion of 1745. He then returned to Scotland and after the battle of Colloden fled to the Highlands, where, from the summit of a lofty eminence, he witnessed the burning of his own proud castle of Dounie, laid in ashes by the royal army.

A fugitive, he wandered from place to place, until arrested on a little island in Loch Moras, near the west coast of Scotland. Thence he was taken to London, where, after a trial lasting five days, he was sentenced to death and *was executed** on the 9th day of April 1747,* as Ann Bailey always asserted, when *she was five years of age.*

It certainly exhibits a great lack of investigation on the part of those who have written of her, for without exception, they all assert that she was born about the year 1700, and yet they declare that, according to her own statement, she was five years of age when Lord Lovat was executed. Now, the *fact* is, as she stated, that she was five years of age in 1747, and that she was born in 1742.

William P. Buell, in a biographical sketch of Ann Bailey, published in the *Magazine of Western History,* for April, 1885, says: "Ann Bailey was born in Liverpool, England, in the year 1700, and was named in honor of Queen Anne, and was present with her parents at her coronation in 1705." This is evidently incorrect, for Anne *was not crowned in 1705,* as stated, but in 1702. Again he says: "At the age of thirty, she married a man named John Trotter." Here he is wrong again; first, in that her husband's name was not *John* but Richard. Now, that we may see how inaccurate such statements are — and the author quoted has followed all of his predecessors — let us admit as true the statement that she married at the age of thirty. Now, if she was born in the year 1700, as asserted, then she was married in 1730. Then her only son was born *thirty–seven* years after her marriage when she was *sixty–seven* years of age, for it is a matter of record that he was born in the year 1767. Then again, accepting the statement that she was born in 1700, she was then seventy–four years of age when left a widow, lived in a state of widowhood eleven years, married John Bailey at the age of *eighty–five* and made her famous ride from Fort Clendenin to Lewisburg, a distance of one hundred miles, continuing night and day, when she was *ninety–one* years old. Is the student of history asked to believe that which is contrary to nature and to the facts of history? No, it cannot be so. Then let Ann Bailey's

---

Publisher's Note: *Lord Lovat was beheaded at age 80. His was the last public execution in England.* [1]

testimony stand as authority; and when she says she was *five* years of age when Lord Lovat was executed, let it be recorded that she was born in Liverpool, England, in 1742.

CHAPTER III.

ANN BAILEY'S MARRIAGE AND RESIDENCE IN THE COLONY OF VIRGINIA.

How or when Ann Bailey came to Virginia, is not certainly known, but notwithstanding this, various statements have been made, each asserted to be true. Mr. Buell, before cited, says that: "When a school girl at the age of nineteen, she was kidnapped with her books while on her way to school, brought to America and landed in Virginia, on James River, where she was sold to defray the expense of her passage."

Certainly, this is not a reasonable statement, for it is not at all probable that those who kidnapped her and brought her across the Atlantic would then have permitted her to be sold into the bondage of others to defray her ship's fare. No authority is given for the statement, presumably, for the reason that there is none.

Mr. Averill, following others, says that: "She wedded Richard Trotter, with whom she sought a home in the province of Virginia. Because of their extreme poverty, both were 'sold out,' as was then the custom, to defray the expense of their passage. They were bought by a gentleman of the name of Bell, residing in Augusta County, Virginia, where, after their term of service expired, they became settlers."

How inconsistent is this. The date given is 1730, which was undoubtedly about *twelve* years before Ann Bailey was born. Again, "they were bought by a gentleman of the name of Bell residing in

Augusta County." This cannot be true, for every student of Virginia history knows that neither "a gentleman of the name of Bell, nor any other *white man*" had found a home in Augusta county at that time. John Lewis was the first settler in Augusta and he reared his cabin home near Staunton, in 1732. This was two years after they declare Ann Bailey, who with her husband, whom they tell us was a brave English soldier, came to serve out a term of bondage in Augusta. How absurd that a brave English soldier should be *sold out* to defray his passage to an English colony.

Now let us see what are the traditions long popular in Virginia. Ann Bailey spent her childhood days in Liverpool, attended the school in which she learned to read and write, and when she had grown to an adult age, her parents died leaving her with small means, but alone in a great city. Then scarcely knowing what to do, she bethought herself friends, (some say relatives) the Bells in their distant home to which they had gone beyond the sea. Heroine that she was, she determined to follow them, and went on shipboard. The sails were unfurled and the ship stood out on the Irish sea; then the coast line of her native land disappeared from view and later, the blue hills of Ireland faded away in the distance, and thoughts came to her of that far–away land to which she was going and in which she was to leave a name to be remembered, honored and revered long years after she had passed from among the living. In time the capes of Virginia stood out to view, and the ship passed up the James. Then the journey into the wilderness began; the Blue Ridge was passed and the future heroine of the Valley of the Kanawha, in 1761, when in her nineteenth year, found a home and a welcome with the Bells near where Staunton now stands.

Soon after her arrival in Augusta, she became acquainted with Richard Trotter, a brave frontiersman, who was then and had been engaged in defending the border settlements from the incursions of the savages* who were then carrying death and destruction into the beautiful Valley of Shenandoah, even to the base of the Blue Ridge.

---

*__Publisher's Note:__ *Statements such as these, considered prejudicial today, are indicative of social attitudes and the writing style of the late 1800s.*

Amid wild solitudes he had grown to manhood, and nature had made him a nobleman; his manners were rough, like the scenes around him, his mind strong, and his disposition grand and fearless. From his earliest childhood he was saluted with the story of savage warfare, and the recital aroused within him a spirit of adventure and daring and he longed to engage in struggles fierce and wild.

The opportunity soon came. In the spring of 1755, General Edward Braddock arrived at Alexandria, Virginia, with an army composed of the 44th and 48th Royal Infantry Regiments, destined for American service. This force proceeded up the Potomac and at Fort Cumberland — now Cumberland City, Maryland — was joined by a regiment of Virginia Provincials, in the ranks of which were many Valley men, one of them being Richard Trotter, then a mere youth.

The march into the wilderness began. Slowly the splendid pageant moved on, the long lines of scarlet uniforms contrasting strangely with the verdure of the forest, while strains of martial music filled the air — sounds so strange beneath the dark shades of the American forest.

It was the evening of the 8th of July, 1755, when the English columns, for the second time reached the Monongahela at a point — now Braddock's Field — ten miles distant from Fort Duquesne. On the next day a crossing was effected, and once across the stream, the order to advance was given, but the columns were scarcely in motion when Gordon, one of the English engineers, saw the French and Indians bounding through the forest. At once a deadly fire was poured in upon the English, who returned it with little effect. Braddock formed the regulars into squares, as if he had been maneuvering on the fields of Europe, and thus the men were shot down in heaps. Of the twelve hundred who crossed the Monongahela, sixty-seven officers and seven hundred and fourteen privates were either killed or wounded. Braddock was among the fallen, and of all his aides, Washington alone was left. Many Virginians were among the dead, but a sufficient number were left — among them Richard Trotter — to form a line and cover the retreat of the shattered army back to Fort Cumberland, whence the Virginians returned to their homes, Richard Trotter going to his, which was near Staunton, where representatives of the family now reside.

Years went by and there came from overseas a maid with fair complexion, hazel eyes, a perfectly developed form, a sweet disposition, a mind strong and vigorous, softened by the rudiments of an education obtained in the schools of Liverpool. It was Ann Hennis. Richard Trotter became enamored of her charms. But "none but the brave deserve the fair;" and none but the brave could win the heart of Ann Hennis, for, through her veins coursed the blood of a father who had served his country long and well, who had marched under the banner of Queen Anne, to many bloody and chaotic fields, and no coward could win the affections of his daughter, even though she was a stranger on the frontier wilds of Virginia. But Richard Trotter had long been engaged in the wars of civilization against barbarism, and in him she beheld a soldier, a hero. This was enough. He had defended the homes of others, he would defend his own. There was a pioneer wedding, and Richard Trotter and Ann Hennis, in the year 1765, were made husband and wife.

CHAPTER IV.

THE AUGUSTA HOME AND THE BATTLE OF POINT PLEASANT — DEATH OF RICHARD TROTTER.

A little cabin was reared and to it Richard Trotter took his happy bride. That home was like all others on the Virginia frontier at that day. A clearing of a few acres was made by cutting away the primeval forest which overshadowed the land, the rude cabin was erected, and then the family moved and though the luxuries of later days were unknown, it became the abode of happiness and contentment, while on all hands was naught but the voiceless wilderness.

Richard Trotter belonged to a class of men of whom it was said: "They are statesmen to–day, farmers to–morrow, and soldiers always." Exposed to a common danger, and sharing alike the toils and privations of the wilderness, they became a distinct class known throughout the Colony as the backwoodsmen of Augusta. They were clad in the border suit of home–spun, made by the hands of wives, mothers, and daughters. Heavy buckskin moccasins and leggins were usually worn, with a hunting shirt and a cap made of beaver or otter skin; the long rifle was carried upon the shoulder; the hatchet was swung in the belt, while the hunting knife was lodged in a sheath fastened to the strap of the shot–pouch. Thus equipped, it is difficult to conceive of a more formidable personage than were these backwoodsmen in full dress, especially when reflecting upon the precision with which they dealt the missiles of death and their wonderful power to endure the fatigue and hardships, incident to a hunter's life. Once upon the route thus prepared, they ranged in summer the valleys beneath the misty forest, or in winter, scaled the summits of the bleak and leafless Alleghenies; and often, after weeks of absence, these backwoodsmen of Augusta returned to their homes to which even Washington, in after years expected to be compelled to fly, there, to defend the last faint spark of liberty.

Beyond the general experience of border life we know nothing of the home life of Richard Trotter and his devoted wife. In the year 1767, two years after their marriage, the bond of union which bound them together was doubly cemented by the birth of a son, who was christened William, and who was to be the chief staff of support to the mother in her declining years.

The storm of savage warfare continued to rage along the western border, but its scenes of blood did not deter these hardy frontiersmen from pushing into the wilderness. Pressing over the mountains, a few of the most adventurous established their homes on Muddy Creek, in the Greenbrier country, but short was the sojourn for this germ of civilization planted in the wilderness, perished by the hands of barbarian fury.*

Time hastened on and brought the year 1774, and with it the close of the halcyon decade of the eighteenth century. The period of Dunmore's War was ushered in. The vast savage aggregation west of the Ohio was pressing down upon the frontier of civilization. Virginia made ready for war and the din of preparation resounded along her borders. Lord Dunmore left the gubernatorial mansion at Williamsburg and, hastening over the Blue Ridge, assisted in mustering an army. Staunton became a rendezvous, and here hundreds of the backwoodsmen of Augusta entered the Colonial army. Among

---

*Publisher's Note: The settlement at Muddy Creek came under ambush by the Shawnee Chief Cornstalk (Keightughqua). Posing as friends, his warriors held a banquet to which, under a peaceful ruse, the settlers were invited. At a given signal, the war party attacked the settlers, killing sixty-five unarmed men, women, and children in a brutally successful trap.[2]

those who plead for volunteers, there was one female voice. It was the wife of Richard Trotter, encouraging the men to strike and break the savage power and thus save the mothers and children of Augusta from the tomahawk and scalping–knife of the savage.

On a bright September morning long lines of sturdy men filed away into the wilderness, and that night, there were many lonely homes throughout Augusta, for the father was gone on the fated march and the shadows of evening gathered thick around the little cabin in which alone were the heroic mother and little son.

The army augmented to eleven hundred men, left Camp Union — now Lewisburg — and began the toilsome march of one hundred and sixty miles to the Ohio. There was not even a track through the rugged mountains, but the gallant army moved through the home of the wolf, the bear and the panther, and beneath the autumnal shades of the forest in which the golden hue of the linden and the maple blended with the crimson of the sumac, and sombre green of the laurel and hemlock, and at last left the rocky mountain tops behind and descended to where the Kanawha and Elk united, widens into fertile bottoms.

The Elk was passed, the march continued and on the first day of October, 1774, the army reached the mouth of the Kanawha, where, on the 10th of the same month, it waged the most fiercely contested battle ever fought with the Indians in Virginia if not on the continent. Indeed, in many aspects, it has no parallel in the annals of forest warfare. That evening as the sun sank behind the low hills of the western wilderness, one hundred and forty wounded Virginians were borne by more fortunate companions into the encampment, while the dead lay scattered over the bloody field. Among the latter was Richard Trotter who, like those who had fallen beside him, had yielded up his life in defense of pioneer homes and in an effort to plant civilization in the Ohio Valley. Such was the scene that October evening at Point Pleasant:

> " *Where all day long the sound of battle rolled;*
> *Where all day long, the fearful and the bold*
> *Behind their slender bulwarks, stern and pale,*

Stood face to face beneath the leaden hail;
Stood face to face, the white man and the red,
Their cause the same, the same their gory bed."

But how different was the scene far away amid the hills of Augusta! That night as the survivors sat amid the dead and dying at Point Pleasant,

"They thought of dear ones far across the hills,
Of West Augusta homes, where warm and bright
The fire–light gleamed on household gods at night,
And dawn awoke each weary, weary day,
When bright eyes waiting, watched the western way,
For forms those eyes might never, never greet;
For forms then stark in death — where two great rivers meet."

Yes, long they watched the western way and at last a message came with the tidings of death, and there was grief and mourning in many Augusta homes. Among them was that of Richard Trotter, where dwelt his widow and orphan son.

CHAPTER V.

A REMARKABLE CAREER OF FEMALE HEROISM – ELEVEN YEARS OF WIDOWHOOD – HER SECOND MARRIAGE.

Wedded at the age of twenty–three, Ann Trotter was a widow at the age of thirty–two, and so remained for eleven years. From the moment she heard of her husband's death, what appeared to be a strange wild dream seemed to possess her, and she resolved to avenge his death. It was far from a visionary dream with her. It was instead the outburst and exhibition of patriotism and heroism combined, as true as was ever evidenced by womankind. No people had ever occupied such a position as those by whom she was surrounded and among whom she lived. The Revolution was now at hand and they were menaced alike by the savage from the wilderness and the Briton from the sea. To the backwoodsmen of the Shenandoah Valley, it was not a war for liberty but of existence as well, and never was a rallying cry more needed than there.

But what could Ann Trotter do? She could not command an army nor bear arms in the wilderness or on the Atlantic seaboard. Then with a fatherless son, but seven years of age, what was there for her to do? But she found a field of duty and tradition tells how well she performed her part.

Her near neighbor was Mrs. Moses Mann, some of whose family had fallen victim to savage barbarity and to her Ann Trotter explained her plans of operation. Mrs. Mann, imbued with a similar spirit, approved all and tendered a home to the little son, made orphan by a savage bullet at Point Pleasant, and the mother at once entered upon a career which has no parallel in Virginia annals.

Clad in the costume of the border she hastened away to the recruiting stations where she urged enlistments with all the earnestness which her zeal and heroism inspired. Her appeals were first in behalf of the defenseless women and children of the border, who were constantly exposed to the attacks of the savages, and when these were not in immediate danger, her voice was heard, urging men to enlist in the Virginia lines on Continental establishment and strike for freedom in a struggle waged against the Land that gave her birth and in which her parents slept the last long sleep.

Clad in buckskin pants, with petticoat, heavy brogan shoes, a man's coat and hat, a belt about the waist in which was worn the hunting–knife, and with rifle on her shoulder, she went from one recruiting station to another and from one muster to another, making her appeals to all whom she met. The whole border, from the Potomac to the Roanoke, was her field of action, and long ere the Revolution closed, the name of Ann Trotter was famous along the border, and her virtue and heroism were extolled by all who knew her.

At last the Briton was gone. Virginia and her sister colonies were free, but for long years to come, the struggle on the western border was to continue and in this, she now redoubled her energy and afoot or mounted on horseback, she bore messages between Staunton and the distant frontier forts, among them Fort Fincastle on Jackson's River, Fort Edward on the Warm Spring Mountain, and Fort Loudoun, now Winchester.

In 1778, Fort Savannah — now Lewisburg, in Greenbrier — was erected and became the most western outpost of civilization, on the southwestern frontier of Virginia, with the single exception of Fort Randolph at Point Pleasant, on the distant banks of the Ohio, and far out in the unbroken wilderness. The former became a favorite objective point for her, and she soon was familiar with every path between Staunton and Lewisburg, along which she bore messages, carried letters, and Staunton awaited her coming with anxiety, for she was a messenger from out the wilderness.

A new field for adventure opened before her. One hundred and sixty miles lay between Lewisburg and Point Pleasant; over the route the army had marched in 1774, and Ann Trotter, no doubt animated by a desire to visit the scene on which crumbled to dust, all that was mortal of her husband, pushed into the wilderness, traversed the lonely defiles of the Allegheny mountains, crossed the Gauley and the Elk, and reached Point Pleasant. Thus she traversed the Valley which was later to be the scene of many of her adventures.

Once more she thought of love and of a fixed habitation. A *soldier* sought her heart and hand. It was John Bailey and he was one worthy of the prize he sought. Long years he had been in service on the frontier and was at that time engaged with a body of scouts, in defending the Roanoke and Catawba settlements from savage hands. Among his associates were James Bailey, Edward Burgess, John Crockett, James Martin, John Maxwell, Oliver Wynn, and James Witten. They with others were the rangers of Southwest Virginia and for years they traversed the valleys of the Big Sandy and its tributaries with those of the Holstein and Upper Tennessee. For such a responsible position, only the best men on the border were chosen, for it will readily appear that one faithless spy might have permitted the Indians to pass unobserved along their warpath, when they would have spread carnage and death throughout the settlement before they could have prepared for defense. But it does not appear that even one of these scouts failed to give the alarm and thus save those whose lives they had in their keeping.

These RANGERS always went together and often remained out several weeks upon the scout. Great caution was necessary to prevent the Indians from discovering them; hence their beds were of leaves in the underbrush, or beneath some shelving rock, whence they could overlook the war–path. Scorched by the summer sun; chilled by the wintry blast, drenched by the driving rain, and pelted by the sleet and hail, these faithful guardians were ever at their posts and with unwearied eye, watched the western way from the heights of the Cumberland and the defiles of the Alleghenies.

What services were performed by these Rangers, led by a Bailey, a Lewis, a McClenachan, a Cunningham, a Preston, a Dickinson, a

Clendenin, a Dunlap, or a Moffett, armed and equipped at their own expense, as they marched into the wilderness to punish or disperse hostile bodies of Indians!

There was no engagement ring. There were no embossed, tinted and perfumed wedding invitation cards sent to the friends and relatives of the contracting parties, but there was a wedding at Lewisburg. There was a minister in readiness, whose name will never be lost from the church annals of West Virginia. It was the Rev. John McCue, the first settled Presbyterian minister west of the Alleghenies. He was licensed to preach May 22, 1782, at Timber Ridge Church, in Rockbridge County, and was instructed by Hanover Presbytery to labor in Greenbrier County. Here his pastorate continued more than nine years. Who composed the wedding guests we do not know, but it was a "marriage in high life" and doubtless many of the Pioneers of Greenbrier were there. We may suppose that in the assembly were the scholarly John Stewart, the heroic Andrew Donnally, with representatives from the McClung, Renick, Hamilton families and others. The date was November 3, 1785, when the bride was forty–three years of age. The minister pronounced them man and wife and thus Ann *Trotter*, the heroine of the Shenandoah Valley, became Ann *Bailey*, the heroine of the Great Kanawha Valley. The record of the marriage may be seen in Marriage Record No. 1, page 7, in the County Clerk's office at Lewisburg.

CHAPTER VI.

REMOVAL TO CLENDENIN'S FORT —
MILITARY AFFAIRS IN THE KANAWHA VALLEY.

Under Governor Dinwiddie's proclamation, of 1754, Colonel Thomas Bullitt received a patent for one thousand and thirty acres of land where Charleston now stands, in 1773. Soon after he sold it to his brother, Cuthbert Bullitt, of Maryland, who in time transferred the title to his son, Cuthbert, of Prince William county.

Prominent on the frontier of Virginia, were the Clendenins, an old Scotch–Irish family. The exact date at which they came to Virginia is a matter of uncertainty, but that they were residing upon "Burden's Grant" as early as 1753, is shown by the records of Augusta County, where the family was founded by two brothers, Archibald and Charles. A third brother came to America but settled at Baltimore, where he became the ancestor to the Clendenins of Maryland. Those in Virginia became daring frontiersmen, satisfied only with a home on the confines of civilization, and this desire to penetrate the wilderness led to the extinction of one branch of the family, Archibald and his family — with the exception of his wife, who escaped from captivity — all perished in the Greenbrier massacre of 1763. It is believed that the other brother, Charles, was married before coming to Virginia. The date at which he removed west of the mountains is not known, but that he with his wife and sons, George, William,

Robert, and Alexander, and daughter, Ellen Mary, was residing on Greenbrier River, as early as 1780, is a matter of record.

George, the eldest son, had risen to prominence in both the civil and military affairs of the state and in 1787, when in Richmond, he met young Bullitt from whom he purchased the lands lying on the Kanawha at the mouth of the Elk, and there in 1788, he removed, taking with him his aged father and brothers and sister, the mother being dead. Here these founders of the future capital of West Virginia, reared the walls of a blockhouse, afterwards known on the frontier as Clendenin's Fort, but it should be Fort Lee, for so it was named in honor of Governor Henry Lee of Virginia.

Here then was another fort to be garrisoned, and to it John Bailey went on duty, taking with him to reside therein, his now famous bride.

Here our heroine entered upon a career unsurpassed in deeds of daring and adventure, in the annals of the whole western border. Her skill with the rifle, the dexterity of equestrian performance, and her care for the sick and helpless, challenged the admiration of the entire garrison and won for her a name still cherished by the descendants of these old soldiers.

Often she left the fort and rode away into the forest and, if the commander wished to send a message to Fort Randolph at the mouth of the Kanawha, distant sixty miles away, Ann Bailey became the messenger, and passing the Elk she disappeared in the wilderness, and down the Kanawha, over streams, through dense underbrush, sleeping if need be, with a horse tied to a tree, and her ears saluted by the howl of the wolf, the scream of the panther or perchance the warwhoop of the savage. Back over the same route, she came bringing the report from the commandant at Point Pleasant.

These were times that tried men's souls, and only the love of helpless wives and babes moved these frontiersmen to deeds, the performance of which has won for them, names as lasting as heroism itself.

More than a century has passed away, and official records are now our only guide to the condition of affairs then existing in the Valley.

April 15, 1790, Thomas Lewis, at the mouth of the Great

Kanawha, wrote Col. George Clendenin, at "Charles Town" — now
Charleston — and said: "It is unnecessary to mention anything
respecting the situation other than that they (the people) are collected
in bodies and await the moment when the savages make a formidable
attack to depopulate the settlements on the Kanawha." Col.
Clendenin forwarded the letter to the Virginia war department by
private carrier.

The central figure in the military affairs at that time, was Col.
George Clendenin. As colonel–commandant of Kanawha County, he
was commander–in–chief of the Valley Department. As such, on
January 1 — New Year's Day — 1791, he addressed a letter to Governor Randolph, relative to the western defenses, in which he said: "I
beg leave to request the honorable board to consider the peculiar
situation of the county of Kanawha — then including the entire
Valley — and the disposition the Indians have lately exercised against
it and that you and the board will indulge the county with four
scouts, in case the general government may not make such arrange-
ments as the exposed situation may require. This number, I am
certain, is not sufficient, but they would be of great service to alarm
the inhabitants of the approach of the enemy, so as to enable them to
collect together to secure themselves from savage cruelty. I feel myself
disposed to make this last request from the most tender motives of
affection for my own family and the lives of my friends and neighbors
equally exposed."

On the 12th day of December, 1791, Daniel Boone, the founder
of Kentucky, but then residing in the Valley and holding the position
of Lieutenant–Colonel of Kanawha County, wrote Governor Henry
Lee, regarding the military establishment of the county. His letter is
characteristic of the man who wrote it:

> "For Kanaway County, 68 Privits; Lenard Cuper, Captain, at
> Pint plesent, 17 men; John Morris, Juner, Insine at the Bote
> yards 17 men. Two spyes or scutes Will be Nessesry at the pint
> to sarch the Banks of the River at the Crossing places. More
> would be Wanting if the(y) could be aloude. Those Spyes Must
> be Compoused of the inhabitence who Well Know the Woods

and Waters from the pint to belleville, 60 mildes —
No inhabitence; also from the pint to Elke, 60 mildes —
No inhabitence; from Elke to the Bote yards, 20 mildes, all
inhabited."

Here we are officially informed that in the year 1791, there was
not a white inhabitant in all the Kanawha Valley, from Point Pleasant
to Fort Charleston, while from the same source we learn that at that
time the cabin homes of the pioneers dotted the banks of the
Kanawha from the last named place to the "Bote yards" by which
Boone refers to the mouth of Kelley's Creek.

Amid such trying scenes, lived the first settlers of the Valley, and
who that looks backward over the lapse of a century, does not fondly
cherish all that pertains to their memory?

CHAPTER VII.

SCENE AT FORT CHARLESTON – ANN BAILEY'S RIDE – SHE SAVES THE GARRISON FROM MASSACRE – HER SECOND WIDOWHOOD.

Let the mind go backward just a hundred years, to 1791, and view the site on which Charleston, with its busy scenes and cultured population, now stands.

There are the same plains, valleys and hills; the same rivers flowed calmly on then as now. In the forests that overhung the banks, the buds had bursted and the green leaves betokened the advance of summer. The beautiful Kanawha, fresh from its mountain springs flowed on in its majesty, as yet its waters unstained by the murky tide of the Ohio. The stately forest on the broad bottoms was so dense that it almost shut out the light of day, while the trunks of the giant trees were festooned with the ivy and the honeysuckle, and the boughs entwined with the grape. On every hand rose the verdant hills, like towers, the work of no human hands, and on their fertile slopes, among the hazel and the alder, flowered the blue–bells and bleeding–hearts.

Amid this scene of inspiring beauty, down close by the brink of the Kanawha, stood Fort Lee. Day unto day the agents of civilization found refuge within its walls. Night came and they repeated the story of struggles fierce and wild; then watched the silent heat lightning which veiled the western sky, or solacing themselves with pipes, listened to the mournful cry of the whippoorwill and the quavering scream of the owl. Then all slept save the lone sentry, whose practical eye pierced the gloomy recesses of the forest, and whose ear caught the slightest sound, even that of the stealthy tread of the wolf and panther.

Suddenly an alarm was given that was terrible enough to quicken the pulsations of the calmest heart: A large body of savages hovered near. The garrison prepared for defense and siege; but lo! a discovery was made that intensified the alarm into terror. The supply of powder in the magazine was almost exhausted, and if an attack should be made, surrender and death at the hand of a savage foe was inevitable.

A hundred miles lay between Fort Lee and Lewisburg — the only place from which a supply of powder could come. Col. George Clendenin summoned the garrison together and called for volunteers, for *men* who would risk their own lives, in an effort to save others. Not one would enter upon the perilous journey. Brave men looked back the dismay which appalled the entire garrison. Then was heard in a determined tone the words "I WILL GO," and every inmate of that beleaguered fort recognized the voice of Ann Bailey.

The fleetest horse within the stockade was caparisoned and brought out. The commander assisted the daring rider to mount. The gate was opened and horse and rider disappeared in the forest, leaving suspense and deferred hope within the fort. Onward she sped up the Kanawha. Gauley was crossed; Kanawha's Falls left in the distance, and onward rode Ann Bailey through the voiceless forest. The Hawk's Nest appeared in sight, and from its summit her eye traced the silvery course of the New River, which, rolling like a destiny, rushed onward through the realms of solitude and shade. Darkness and day were one to her; she knew the route; it was a ride for life and there could be no stop. The shadows of night were lifted; the Greenbrier Mountains stood out against the eastern sky; the forests on the Lewisburg hills glistened in the morning sunlight, and the walls of Fort Savannah rose to view. A familiar voice; an opening of the gates; a welcome, and Ann Bailey was telling to the commandant the condition of affairs at Fort Lee and the object of her mission.

The delay was short. She was furnished with an additional horse and both were laden with powder. The officer in command offered to send a guard with her but this she declined and with the two horses, the one rode, the other lead — she began her perilous return. Night and day she pressed on, and at last, well nigh exhausted, but animated by the hope of saving others' lives, she reached Fort Lee, and amid shouts, the echoes of which died away among the surrounding hills, she was ushered within the gates, having accomplished the most daring feat recorded in the annals of the West. The savages still hovered near, but the next morning, the garrison sallied forth and after a spirited action, forced them to raise the siege and thus that feeble garrison on the site where a capital city now stands, was saved from savage butchery, and that too, by the Heroine of the Great Kanawha Valley. She was then in the forty–ninth year of her age.

The poet has sung of the deed of Elizabeth Zane who dared a storm of savage bullets at Fort Henry, but that was a life imperiled but for a moment, and who shall say that the achievement of Ann Bailey was not a far greater undertaking, for in addition to the danger of the long perilous ride, she left Fort Lee and returned to it under a savage fire.

Her deed has been commemorated in song as well as story. Charles Robb, of the United States Army was at Gauley Bridge, in 1861, and having heard the story of Ann Bailey, wrote the following, which at the time appeared in the Clermont (Ohio) *Courier*.

ANN BAILEY'S RIDE
A LEGEND OF THE KANAWHA.
by Charles Robb, United States Army

> The Army lay at Gauley Bridge,
> At Mountain Cove and Sewell Ridge;
> Our tents were pitched on hill and dell
> From Charleston Height to Cross Lane fell;
> Our camp–fires blazed on every route,
> From Red House point to Camp Lookout;
> On every rock our sentries stood,
> Our scouts held post in every wood,

And every path was stained with blood
From Scarey Creek to Gauley flood.

" 'Twas on a bleak autumnal day,
When not a single sunbeam's ray
Could struggle through the dripping skies
To cheer our melancholy eyes —
Whilst heavy clouds, like funeral palls,
Hung o'er Kanawha's foaming falls,
And shrouded all the mountain green
With dark, foreboding, misty screen.

All through the weary livelong day
Our troops had marched the mountain way;
And in the gloomy eventide
Had pitched their tents by the river's side;
And as the darkness settled o'er
The hill and vale and river shore,
We gathered round the camp–fire bright
That threw its glare on the misty night;

And each some tale or legend told
To while away the rain and cold.
Thus, one a tale of horror told
That made the very blood run cold;
One spoke of suff'ring and of wrong;
Another sang a mountain song;
One spoke of home, and happy years,
'Till down his swarthy cheek the tears
Slow dripping, glistened in the light
That glared upon the misty night;
While others sat in silence deep,
Too sad for mirth, yet scorned to weep.

Then spake a hardy mountaineer —
(His beard was long, his eye was clear;
And clear his voice, of metal tone,
Just such as all would with to own) —

" I've heard a legend old," he said,
" Of one who used these paths to tread
Long years ago, when fearful strife
Sad havoc made of human life;
A deed of daring bravely done,
A feat of honor noble won;
And what in stories most uncommon
An army saved by gentle woman.

" 'Twas in that dark and bloody time
When savage craft and Tory crime
From Northern lake to Southern flood,
Had drenched the western world with blood.
And in this wild, romantic glen
Encamped a host of savage men,
Whose mad'ning war–whoop, loud and high,
Was answered by the panther's cry.

" The pale–faced settlers all had fled,
Or murdered were in lonely bed;
Whilst hut and cabin, blazing high,
With crimson decked the midnight sky.

" I said the settlers all had fled —
Their pathway down the valley led
To where the Elk's bright crystal waves
On dark Kanawha's bosom laves,
There safety sought, and respite brief,
And in Fort Charleston found relief;
Awhile they bravely met their woes,
And kept at bay their savage foes.

" Thus days and weeks the warfare waged,
In fury still the conflict raged;
Still fierce and bitter grew the strife
Where every foeman fought for life.
Thus day by day the siege went on,
'Till three long, weary weeks were gone;

And then the mournful word was passed
That every day might be their last;
The word was whispered soft and slow,
The magazine was getting low.
They loaded their rifles one by one,
And then — the powder all was gone!
They stood like men in calm despair,
No friendly aid could reach them there;
Their doom was sealed, the scalping knife
And burning stake must end the strife.
One forlorn hope alone remained,
That distant aid might yet be gained
If trusty messenger should go
Through forest wild, and savage foe,
And safely there should bear report,
And succor bring from distant Fort.

But who should go — the venture dare?
The woodsmen quailed in mute despair,
In vain the call to volunteer;
The bravest blenched with silent fear.
Each gloomy brow and labored breath,
Proclaimed the venture worse than death.
Not long the fatal fact was kept;
But through the Fort the secret crept
Until it reached the ladies's hall,
There like a thunderbolt to fall.
Each in terror stood amazed,
And silent on the other gazed;
No word escaped — there fell no tear —
But all was hushed in mortal fear;
All hope of life at once had fled,
And filled each soul with nameless dread.
But one who stood amid the rest,
The bravest, fairest, and the best
Of all that graced the cabin hall,

First broke the spell of terror's thrall.
Her step was firm, her features fine,
Of Mortal mould the most divine;
But why describe her graces fair,
Her form, her mien, her stately air?
Nay, hold! my pen, I will not dare!
'Twas Heaven's image mirrored there.
She spoke no word, of fear, or boast,
But smiling, passed the sentry post;
And half in hope, and half in fear,
She whispered in her husband's ear,
The sacrifice her soul would make
Her friends to save from brand and stake.
A noble charger standing nigh,
Of spirit fine, and metal high,
Was saddled well, and girted strong,
With cord, and loop, and leathern thong,
For her was led in haste from stall,
Upon whose life depended all.
Her friends she gave a parting brief,
No time was there for idle grief;
Her husband's hand a moment wrung,
Then lightly to the saddle sprung;
And followed by the prayers and tears,
The kindling hopes, and boding fears
Of those who seemed the sport of fate,
She dashed beyond the op'ning gate;
Like birdling free, on pinion light,
Commenced her long and weary flight.

"The foeman saw the op'ning gate,
And thought with victory elate
To rush within the portal rude,
And in his dark and savage mood
To end the sanguinary strife
With tomahawk and scalping–knife.

But lo! a lady! fair and bright,
And seated on a charger light,
Bold — and free — as one immortal —
Bounded o'er the op'ning portal.
Each savage paused in mute surprise,
And gazed with wonder–staring eyes;
'A squaw! a squaw!' the chieftain cries,
('A squaw! a squaw!' the host replies):
Then order gave to 'cross the lawn
With lightning speed and catch the fawn.'
Her pathway up the valley led,
Like frightened deer the charger fled,
And urged along by whip and rein,
The quick pursuit was all in vain,
A hundred bended bows were sprung,
A thousand savage echoes rung —
But far too short the arrows fell
All harmless in the mountain dell;
'To horse! to horse!' the chieftain cried,
They mount in haste and madly ride.
Along the rough, uneven way,
The pathway of the lady lay;
Whilst long and loud the savage yell
Re–echoed through the mountain fell.
She heeded not the dangers rife,
But rode as one who rides for life;
Still onward in her course she bore
Along the dark Kanawha's shore,
Through tangled wood and rocky way,
Nor paused to rest at close of day.
Like skimming cloud before the wind
Soon left the rabble far behind.
From bended tree above the road
The flying charger wildly trode,
Amid the evening's gath'ring gloom,
The panther's shriek, the voice of doom

In terror fell upon the ear,
And quickened every pulse with fear.
But e'en the subtle panther's bound,
To reach his aim too slow was found;
And headlong falling on the rock,
Lay crushed and mangled in the shock.
The prowling wolf then scents his prey,
And rushing on with angry bay,
With savage growl and quickening bound
He clears the rough and rugged ground;
And closing fast the lessening space
That all too soon must end the race,
With sharpened teeth that glittered white
As stars amid the gloomy night —
With foaming jaws had almost grasped
The lovely hand that firmly clasped,
And well had used the whip and rein,
But further effort now were vain;
Another bound — a moment more —
And then the struggle all were o'er.
'Twas in a steep and rocky gorge
Along the river's winding verge,
Just where the foaming torrent falls
Far down through adamantine halls.
And then comes circling round and round,
As loth to leave the enchanted ground.
Just there a band of wand'ring braves
Had pitched their tents beside the waves.
The sun long since had sunk to rest,
And long the light had faded west —
When all were startled by the sound
Of howling wolf and courser's bound,
That onward came, with fearful clang,
Whose echoes round the mountain rang;
The frightened wolf in wild surprise
A moment paused — with glaring eyes

In terror gazed upon the flame,
The backward fled the way he came.
Each wondering savage saw with fear
The charger come like frightened deer;
With wary gait, and heavy tramp,
The foaming steed dashed through the camp
And onward up the valley bear
His gueenly rider, brave and fair.
Still on, and on, through pathless wood —
They swim the Gauley's swollen flood,
And climb Mount Tompkins' lofty brow,
More wild and rugged far than now,
Still onward held their weary flight
Beyond the Hawk's Nest's giddy height;
And often chased through lonely glen
By savage beast or savage men —
Thus like some weary, hunted dove
The woman sped through 'Mountain Cove',
The torrent crossed without a bridge,
And scaled the heights of Sewell Ridge,
And still the wild, beleaguered road
With heavy tramp the charger trode,
Nor paused amid his weary flight
Throughout the long and dreary night.
And bravely rode the woman there,
Where few would venture, few would dare
Amid the cheering light of day
To tread the wild beleaguered way;
And as the morning sunbeams fall
O'er hill and dale, and sylvan hall,
Far in the distance, dim and blue,
The friendly Fort* arose to view,
Whose portal soon the maiden gains
With slackened speed and loosened reins

*Lewisburg

And voice whose trembling accents tell,
Of journey ridden long and well.

"The succor thus so nobly sought,
To Charleston Fort was timely brought;
Whilst Justice, on the scroll of fame,
In letters bold, engraved her name."

GAULEY BRIDGE, VA., NOV. 7, 1861.

The generation in which she lived could not repay her for the service rendered, but the garrison at Fort Lee, in appreciation thereof, promptly, on her return, voted her a present of the horse on which she had made the daring ride. He was a fine animal, black, with white fee, blazed face and glassy eyes. She named him "Liverpool," in honor of her birthplace in England, and he was thenceforth to be associated with her in many adventures.

A brief notice of the road on which the daring ride was made must prove of interest. Colonel John Stuart of Greenbrier, in a Memoir, written in 1798, thus tells of its construction:

"The paper money emitted for maintaining our war against the British became totally depreciated, and there was not a sufficient quantity of specie in circulation to enable the people to pay the revenue tax assessed upon the citizens of this county (Greenbrier), wherefore we fell in arrears to the public for four years. But the Assembly again taking our remote situation under consideration, graciously granted the sum of five thousand pounds of our said arrears to be applied to the purpose of opening a road from Lewisburg to the Kanawha River. The people, grateful for such indulgence, willingly embraced the opportunity of such an offer, and every person liable for arrears of tax agreed to perform labor equivalent on the road, and the people being formed into districts with each a superintendent, the road was completed in the space of two months in the year 1786, and thus was a communication by wagon to the

navigable waters of the Kanawha first effected, and which will probably be found the nighest and best conveyance from the Eastern to
the Western country that will ever be known."

It is thus seen that the road had been constructed *five* years before
Ann Bailey made her historic journey over it.

The writer is unable to learn the exact date of the death of her
husband, John Bailey, but it is believed to have occurred about the
year 1802, at Charleston or in the vicinity. He owned a tract of land
in the Kanawha County, situated on the headwaters of Campbell's,
Blue, Bell, and Kelley's Creeks, but it passed into the possession of
John Barkley in 1802, and the name of John Bailey disappeared from
the assessor's books after that date. He was buried on the Joseph
Carroll farm, fifteen miles above Charleston, on an eminence overlooking the beautiful Kanawha, and there his remains now repose.

CHAPTER VIII.
THE PEOPLE AMONG WHOM ANN BAILEY LIVED.

The Treaty of Greenville in 1795 forever put an end to savage warfare in the Kanawha Valley and the influences of civilized life spread abroad over its entire extent. Among the pioneers, Ann Bailey spent many years and grew old among them. Everywhere she was a most welcome guest, and she found a home wherever she stopped. A notice of those long associated with her, if but a mention of their names, must recall pleasant memories.

Colonel George Clendenin and his brothers were the founders of Charleston. Three of them, George, William, and Alexander, were in the Battle of Point Pleasant; the first being then but seventeen years of age. His wife was Geneive McNeale, a sister of the wife of General Thomas Ewing of Ohio.

He had issue a daughter, Parthena, who married first R.J. Meigs of Marietta, Ohio. They removed to Paris, Kentucky where the husband died leaving the widow with one son, R.J. Meigs, who at the age of ninety years, now lives in Washington City. The widow returned to Point Pleasant, where on June 1, 1809, she wedded Andrew Bryan; by whom she had issue four children, the eldest being Mary — now the aged Mrs. Mary McCulloch, of Mason County, who is the nearest living relative of the founder of Charleston. She has an excellent memory, unimpaired by age, and she well remembers Ann

Bailey, she often being a guest at the Bryan home.

William Clendenin, brother of George, left Fort Lee at Charleston in 1797, and settled on the Ohio River nine miles above Point Pleasant; but in 1802, he removed four miles below the mouth of the Kanawha, where he reared his cabin and cleared the first acre of land improved on Mercer's Bottom. Here Ann Bailey, in her later years, often delighted the neighbors with the recital of her adventures.

The garrison at old Fort Randolph had left its walls and were living around Point Pleasant. Among them were John VanBibber, Mathias VanBibber, John Reynolds, Isaac Tyler, Michael See, Benjamin Eulin and Luman Gibbs. The latter was a famous scout. Born in New Hampshire in 1755, he came to Virginia just in time to enlist in the army of General Lewis, and later participated in the Battle of Point Pleasant. He was one of the men detailed to build the fort after the battle. Here he soon became a famous scout, and for twenty long, dark, and bloody years, he served in that capacity; wandering over the neighboring hills with his rifle in his hand and the love of his fellow men in his heart. Rarely was it that the savages reached the Valley, that their movements were not watched by his unwearied eye. Weekly he sallied forth from the fort and proceeded up the Kanawha to the mouth of Eighteen Mile creek; thence through the wilderness to Letart Falls, and thence down the Ohio, to Point Pleasant; where his report of "All is well," dispelled for the time the fear of massacre from those confined within the fort. So well was his route known, that by the early settlers, it was called "Gibb's Trace." He died in 1839 and is buried about eight miles from Point Pleasant. By his side sleep James Ball and Isaac Robinson, soldiers in the battle of Point Pleasant and heroes of the Revolution.

Prominent among those with whom Ann Bailey lived was Captain William Arbuckle. He was born of Scotch-Irish parentage near Balcony Falls on the James River in the year 1746. His entire life and best energies were contributed to wrest this fair domain from the sway of savage men, and his entire life was characterized by noble acts performed in this effort to settle the wilderness. In every walk of life he was as truly great as Daniel Boone or Simon Kenton. When General Lewis was collecting his army at Camp Union, preparatory to the campaign of 1774, William Arbuckle was among the first to enroll his name in Captain Stewart's company, in which he served to the close of Dunmore's War, having distinguished himself on the bloody field at Point Pleasant, and also by his determined opposition to Dunmore after the army reached the Pickaway Plains. He witnessed the murder of Cornstalk at Point Pleasant, November 10, 1777 and risked his life to prevent it. In 1778, he joined the expedition of Colonel Clarke against the British posts in Illinois and Indiana, the most remarkable military movement recorded in the history of the West. Three hundred men entered upon the march of 600 miles, through a trackless wilderness. After many days toiling through almost impassable swamps, the waters of which were in many places waist deep, they reached their destination and by stratagem, succeeded in surprising and capturing three of the strongest fortifications in the West. Returning to the Valley, we find him by the side of his brother Mathew, Captain John Stuart, Jesse VanBibber, and others defending the settlements against the incursions of the Indians. Soon after he came to the Kanawha, he wedded Catherine, the beautiful and accomplished widow of Captain Robert McClenahan who fell at Point Pleasant. She was a cousin of James Madison, fourth president of the United States. After their marriage, they settled at Fort Savannah — now Lewisburg — in which Jane, who subsequently became the wife of Joseph McMullin, was born. Removing to Point Pleasant, he had two daughters born in Fort Randolph. When the war was over he settled on the Kanawha, four miles below where Buffalo now stands, where both he and his wife lived to a ripe old age; and when they had seen their children well settled in life, and the wilderness blossom as the rose, and had seen the transit of palatial steamers on the Kanawha, and when churches and school houses had been reared about them, then they died and found a grave nearby where they had found a home. Ann Bailey was ever a welcome guest in their hospitable home.

Daniel Boone was also a resident in the Valley. The cause which led to his removal from Kentucky is but another instance of man's injustice to man. Boone had been the first white man to find a home in the wilds of Kentucky; he had discovered its wonderful resources and had proclaimed them to the world. His footsteps had been marked in blood. Two darling sons had fallen by savage hands amid the gloomy defiles of the Allegheny Mountains. Many dark and sleepless nights he had been the companion of wild beasts, separated from the society of civilized men, scorched by the summer's sun and chilled by the winter's blast — he was an instrument ordained to settle the wilderness. When the storm of war had died away and Boone had settled upon his lands, the sheriff suddenly entered the cabin and informed him that the title to his lands was disputed, and that legal proceedings had been instituted against him. Boone could not understand this. Kentucky he regarded as his own by the right of discovery. He had led the way there; he had established himself and family in the land and now, in his advancing years, to be driven from that home seemed unjust indeed. He made no defense, and, stung by ingratitude, he turned his eyes to the distant home of his childhood on the Schuylkill, from which he had wandered forty years before. But there, all was changed and amid blooming orchards and culti-vated fields, there could be no home for him. Forever leaving the scene, he came to the Kanawha Valley, where he found congenial spirits with whom he spent ten or twelve years of his life. With George Clendenin he represented Kanawha County in the general assembly of Virginia in 1791, and about the year 1798, sought and found a home with his son, Daniel M. Boone, in the wilds of Upper Louisiana. There he died in 1820, and in 1845, his remains were removed to Frankfort, Kentucky, where they now repose.

Then there was Captain Jesse VanBibber, who, when the wars were past, built his cabin on Thirteen Mile Creek, now in Mason County. He was the first settler on that stream. His early life, like the mountain stream on which he settled, was rough in the extreme. Born on the frontier, he early in life became inured to hardships and privations experienced only by pioneers of the wilderness. The bloody scenes in which the tomahawk and scalping knife played prominent parts were those with which he had grown familiar, having witnesses the murder and scalping of his own niece Rhoda VanBibber on the banks of the Ohio River opposite Point Pleasant. He was a soldier during Dunmore's War, serving in the southern wing of the army, when he was eulogized by General Lewis for his bravery displayed on the field at Point Pleasant. From 1774 to 1795 he was constantly engaged in the military affairs of the Valley. His commission as captain is in the archives of the West Virginia Historical and Antiquarian Society. During Boone's sojourn in the Valley, he was often the guest of Captain VanBibber and many times they were companions in the chase. It was on the occasion of one of their hunts on the waters of Thirteen that Boone bestowed the name of "Mud Lick" upon the principal tributary of that stream. Far up it is a lick or salt spring which at that time, was kept muddy constantly by the animals that resorted thither in quest of the brackish waters. Here in the depth of the forest these two pilots of the wilderness spent many a night awaiting the approach of the game which, rarely if ever, failed to become the victims of their deadly rifles. When speaking of this locality, Boone referred to it as the Mud Lick Creek; and long years after, Captain VanBibber informed the settlers as they came in that Boone had named the stream. They were willing that it should retain the name bestowed upon it by the founder of Kentucky, and by that name it is known today. Captain VanBibber, late in life, became a member of the Baptist church, and as his eventful life drew to a close it beautifully reflected the Christian character. He died in 1847 and is buried near where he spent the last years of his life. His home was one of Ann Bailey's favorite stopping places, and here with the old soldier, was the rehearsed the past story of their eventful lives.

Of all the warriors who established homes in the Valley of the Kanawha, none were braver or more honored than the Coopers. Major Leonard Cooper held a commission in the military establishment of Maryland, and when he learned of the westward march of General Lewis, he hastened to Staunton and tendered his services, which were accepted and he participated in the Battle of Point Pleasant. Returning east, he served in a Maryland regiment to the close of the Revolutionary War. In 1785, in company with Thomas Teays and John Turley, he visited Point Pleasant; and on their return up the Valley, the encamped for the night at the mouth of Scarey Creek. In the night their horses strayed away and Cooper and Teays, the next morning, went in search of them. When just below the creek they were fired upon by a party of eight Indians and Teays was killed. Cooper, unhurt, jumped from his horse, crossed the creek and escaped up the mountain. He supposed that Turley was killed at camp for the reason that he heard firing in that direction. This was doubtless true for Turley was never afterward heard of. In 1789 Major Cooper removed with his family to Point Pleasant and, in 1794, erected what was for many years known as "Cooper's Blockhouse." It stood on the north bank of the Kanawha, about nine miles from Point Pleasant, and on lands now owned by George W. Pullins, Esq. Here Major Cooper continued to reside until the time of his death in 1808. When Mason County was formed in 1804, Major Cooper became one of the justices of the new county and as such, continued until his death. During his residence at the mouth of the Kanawha his son Leonard was born. The year was 1791 and he was the first white child born at Point Pleasant. How strong the ties were that bound Ann Bailey to the Cooper family, the sequel will show.

Far down on Mercer's Bottom lived Captain John Hereford. He was one of the earliest settlers in what is now Mason County, coming from Fairfax County, Virginia, in 1790. He was an ardent patriot during the Revolution and for his gallantry on the field on battle, was promoted to the rank of adjutant, serving under Colonels John Alexander and George West, each commanding Virginia regiments; and with the latter, was at the siege of Yorktown. Few men have enjoyed a higher reputation for sterling integrity. In his nature, brave, generous, and magnanimous, he commanded the respect and esteem of those around him. He died May 13, 1846, in the eighty-ninth year of his age. He had been a soldier and certainly Ann Bailey would find a welcome in his home.

There, too, resided Joseph H. Holloway on the farm now owned by John W. Steenbergen. He was from that part of Botetourt, now included in Allegheny, where he wedded Mary Hinton. He was a soldier of the War of 1812. He and his wife had known Ann Bailey long before they came to Mercer's Bottom, and with them she spent much of her time, especially in the later years of her life.

Our heroine was often a visitor at the residence of Dr. Jesse Bennett, six miles up the Ohio River from Point Pleasant. He was born in 1749 in Pennsylvania, near the spot that gave birth to Daniel Boone. Graduating in medicine in Philadelphia, he wedded Elizabeth, the daughter of Peter Hogg, the king's Prosecutor of Dunmore (now Shenandoah) County, in the colony of Virginia. In 1797, in company with his brother-in-law William Hawkins, settled at Six Mile Island, now in Mason County, which he represented in the General Assembly of Virginia in 1808. In 1812 he went, as surgeon, with the Mason County Riflemen to the Maumee. He died in 1842, having been the first regularly educated physician that practiced his profession in the Valley of the Kanawha.

We have not space to notice in detail all of the early settlers with whom Ann Bailey was familiar and at whose hospitable houses she was so often a welcome guest. Among them, in addition to those mentioned on Mercer's Bottom, were: Thomas Hannan, Thomas Powell, Edward S. Menager, John Morris, George Withers, James George, Andrew Wallace, William P. Hereford, Esom Hannan, Bailey Holley, and Reuben Cremeans. Near where Leon now stands lived Jacob Mackley, Theophilus McCoy, Robert Pruit, Michael See, James Ringsbury, Maurice Greenlee, Samuel Smith, Boudridge Warner, Joseph Harrison, and James Nelson. Near the present site of Buffalo were Jonathan Hill, Ira Dilno, and Thomas Scott, while at Charleston and in the vicinity were Joseph, David, and Tobias Ruffner, Fleming Cobb, Mathias VanBibber, Jacob Young, Lewis Tackett, Andrew Donnally, William, Henry, and Leonard Morris, John Reynolds, John Hansford, Paddy Huddlestons, Shadrach Harriman, Robert McKee, John Wilson, and many others. The latter married Catharine, the daughter of Andrew Donnally, the builder and defender of Fort Donnally in Greenbrier, and settled near Springhill, in Kanawha County. He was Captain of the Kanawha Volunteers in the War of 1812. His house was a favorite stopping place for Ann Bailey and there she ever found a hearty welcome.

Beyond the Ohio River, four miles below Point Pleasant at Gallipolis, the representatives of another nation had escaped the horrors of the French Revolution and had found a home on the banks of the Ohio. Joel Barlow in 1790 as the agent of the Scioto Land Company, had appeared in Paris and, in the street Rue Neuve, des

Petits Champs, had offered for sale at a French crown per acre, three million acres of land situated on the Ohio River in what was then the Northwest Territory. Sales were rapidly made, and in 1791 ships left the port of Havre de Grace, having on board large numbers of emigrants bound for the new Canaan on the banks of the Ohio. In time they were landed at Alexandria, Virginia, whence they wended their way over the mountains by way of Winchester, Brownsville, and thence down *la Belle Riviere*; and in the months of October, November, and December, between four and five hundred French emigrants landed at Gallipolis. All was gaiety and music of a high order, for the first time, vibrated through the solitudes of the wilderness. The founders of Gallipolis — the city of the Gauls — were then upon the scene where they laid the foundations of that culture and refinement which has characterized their descendants in later days.*

Soon Ann Bailey was a visitor within the cabins which then adorned what is now the city park. These Frenchmen, and their sons, wives, and daughters heard the story of her life. With them she found a hearty welcome, and thenceforth she was, to the end of her life, a familiar figure on the streets and in the homes of that town.

---

*Publisher's Note: The statement "All was gaiety and music of a high order…" *is somewhat incorrect, for once arriving in Gallipolis, the emigrants found that the deeds were worthless and they had been swindled in a dishonest land deal. Being of a social class possessing money, they found themselves unfit to perform the laborious chores normally handled by the working class, but managed to carve out a successful settlement. The original* French 500, *as they are now known, left few if any known descendants — of those that had not moved away, most were killed by an epidemic of yellow fever carried to Gallipolis on a steamship in the mid-1800s.*[3]

CHAPTER IX.

REMINISCENCES OF ANN BAILEY — HER TWENTY-SEVEN YEARS' RESIDENCE IN THE KANAWHA VALLEY.

After her famous ride from Fort Lee to Lewisburg, Ann Bailey appears to have abandoned all thought of a fixed habitation; and thenceforth, mounted on her favorite horse Liverpool, she ranged all over the country, from Point Pleasant to Staunton.

Surrounded with peace and quiet, her heroism might have slumbered, but contact with the wilderness was a rude touchstone, which developed traits that would have remained dormant, and therefore would have remained unsuspected in civilized life.

She was a tower of adamancy against which hardship, danger, the rage of the savages and of the elements, fatigue, and hunger emptied their quivers in vain. Never under the impenetrable coat of mail of crusader beat a heart actuated by greater heroism and ardent love for humanity than that which throbbed within the breast of Ann Bailey.

She was stranger to fear, and while men were still subjected to garrison duty in the border stockade forts, she boldly sallied forth into the wilderness as if to challenge the ferocity of wild beasts and the vengeance of savage men. Day and night she continued on the journey, and many times slept in the wilderness with only her faithful horse tied nearby.

The rigors of winter had no terrors for her. On one occasion when on a journey from Charleston to Lewisburg, darkness overtook her when amid the storm–swept Alleghenies. It was bitter cold, and to prevent freezing, she sought and found a hollow tree into which she crept and then held her horse so that he constantly blew his breath upon her, and was thus saved from freezing.

Dr. D.C. Forbes, for a number of years a practitioner at Leon, on the Kanawha River, informed the writer several years since, that when he first came to the Valley, there was a cave under a shelving rock on the hillside just below the mouth of Thirteen Mile Creek; it was locally known as "Ann Bailey's Cave," and that he was informed by the old settlers, several of whom were then living, that here she spent many a night. Leaving the fort at Charleston, she would ride this far, find shelter for the night and then proceed to Point Pleasant the next morning. The doctor expressed regret that in his temporary absence, workmen quarried the rock and thus obliterated one of the historic landmarks of the Valley.

It is related that once, when on a journey from Point Pleasant to Charleston, and when a short distance above where Winfield is now situated, she was discovered by a wandering band of savages. They gave chase and she, finding that she would be overtaken, dismounted from her horse and, escaping unto the underbrush, concealed herself in the hollow of a sycamore log. The Indians made extended search for her and halted to rest on the log in which she was concealed, but at length departed, taking her horse with them. Late in the evening she crept forth from her hiding place and, taking the trail of the Indians, followed it until she came in view of their encampment. Then awaiting the cover of darkness, and while they slept, she quietly stole up and untied Liverpool, and sprang upon his back; and when a short distance away, she uttered a scream of defiance and, riding rapidly, reached Charleston in safety. So often did she thus baffle the Indians that they came to believe she was a charmed being. The Shawnee warriors knew her as "The White Squaw of the Kanawha."

First, because of her reckless daring, they believed her to be insane, and they ever regarded one in that condition as being under the special care of the Great Spirit. Then, in their superstition, they beheld her as the "phantom rider," which appeared here, there and everywhere on their paths. They saw her glide through the dark

foliage on the plains of the Kanawha, and from the mountain summits they beheld her as she galloped along the rocky and narrow
defiles of the Alleghenies. To the Indian, everything that he did not
comprehend, was attributed to a supernatural agency, and then he
held it in the greatest awe and reverence. To this fact, Ann Bailey
probably owed her life, for these forest warriors were so much impressed with what seemed to them to be an apparition or phantom
that they feared even an ambush to send the arrow or bullet after her.
Thus rode the "White Squaw of the Kanawha," of whom the Indians
themselves long retained a tradition.

At last the savage no more visited the Valley of the Kanawha, and
when the pioneers practiced war no more, they engaged in the peaceful avocations of civilized life, but for Ann Bailey, there could be no
permanent home. The only home that she could know, was that of
others. The military spirit was so fully developed in her, that to the
day of her death, she continued that adventurous career to her, and
for years, mounted on horseback, she was a conspicuous figure in all
the country from Gallipolis and Point Pleasant to Staunton.

At the former places and along the Kanawha were many families,
who were hundreds of miles from the necessaries of life, not to
mention the conveniences. There were no post offices; not a pound of
coffee, gunpowder, or lead within a hundred miles; and these, if
obtained at all, must be brought from Lewisburg or Staunton.

Here, then, was a field and an occupation for Ann Bailey, and
well did she improve it. From the French at Gallipolis, where she had
become a great favorite, from the dwellers at Point Pleasant and along
the Kanawha, she obtained orders for the articles most in need, and
then rode away to Lewisburg; where she secured them if they were
there to be had. If not, then the journey was extended to Staunton,
from which, with her horse frequently so heavily laden, that she
walked and lead him. Thus was brought to the Valley coffee for one,
drugs for another, powder for another, a farming utensil for another,
and so on through the list of absolute necessities. She frequently
purchased articles when at Staunton of which she made sale in the
Kanawha Valley. The venerable James H. Holloway, of Point Pleasant,
recently informed the writer that he, when a boy, purchased from her

the first pocket-knife he ever owned.

The writer, a few weeks since, asked the aged Mrs. Mary McCulloch of Mason County, who well remembers Ann Bailey, about the business in which she was engaged. In reply, she said: "Oh, yes; she would bring anything that a horse could carry, just like an express company, and she was honest to a cent. Money was scarce and the people could not make change, but no matter what amount they gave Ann Bailey, every cent of it was accounted for."

Think of it! Ann Bailey doing a regular express business in the Kanawha Valley a hundred years ago. She antedated Alvin Adams, Ephraim Farnesworth, and William Harnden by nearly half a century. Who shall say that if she would have had energetic successors who would have continued the business thus begun by her, the Bailey Express Company would not today be one of the greatest public carriers in all the land?

If it were hogs or cattle that were wanted, she drove them through, even if she had to go to the banks of the Shenandoah for them. There is a tradition, current for nearly a hundred years, that she brought the first tame geese to the Kanawha Valley. Captain William Clendenin, soon after his removal to Mercer's Bottom, entered into a contract with her to bring him a number of tame geese from the Greenbrier Valley, where they had been introduced previously from the Shenandoah Valley. The contract was in keeping with the Captain's exact methods of transacting business, and specified that the number should be just *twenty*, else he would not pay for them.

Ann Bailey went to Greenbrier, where she collected the required number and drove them through to the Kanawha. When near Charleston one of the number died, and, remembering the terms of the contract, she dismounted and putting the dead goose in a bag, proceeded on to Clendenin's. Upon her arrival, she drove the flock into the yard. The Captain carefully counted the number and finding that there were but *nineteen*, said: "Well, Ann, you did not bring the number named in the contract and I cannot pay for them."

She, with a business mein equal to that of the Captain, walked out to where she had hitched horse, and taking the *dead* goose from the bag, threw it down in the yard and remarked, "There's your twenty."

The Captain saw where the contract was defective, and promptly paid the bill.

Biography should be a true portraiture of the subject, else it fails of its chief uses in literature, for it is worthless save for the examples it presents. What of the character of Ann Bailey? It has been asserted that she indulged in profanity and drank to intoxication. In an effort to ascertain the truthfulness of this statement, the writer has in the past fifteen years made careful inquiry of more than a dozen persons, all of whom knew her and some of whom are yet living, relative to the moral character of Ann Bailey, and here gives the results:

Mrs. Rebecca Clendenin, formerly of Mason County, now deceased, stated that when a small girl she once went to the house of Captain Clendenin and found him and Ann Bailey engaged in an animated discussion, relative to some past event, while a bottle of brandy sat on the table nearby. They could not agree and it was decided that they should compromise the matter by taking a drink, which they did. Beyond this, no evidence of intoxication has been found. She would take a drink but we must remember that in a new country, a hundred years ago, that was not looked upon by a more polite society. There is no evidence that she ever indulged in profanity.

The aged Mrs. Mary Irions, of Gallia County, Ohio, and a granddaughter of the subject, said to the writer: "Grandma did not belong to any church but she was a good woman. She never used bad language; she carefully observed the Sabbath and many times I have heard her pray."

What more was needed? Heroism, virtue, integrity, mercy, benevolence, observance of the Sabbath and a dependence upon that Providence which had protected her all along an eventful pathway of life, all blended, make up the character of Ann Bailey, the Pioneer Heroine of the Kanawha Valley.

She could not bear the thought of annihilation — of ceasing to exist, and it is related that she frequently gave expression to the thought that in the hereafter, she would rather exist in misery than not to exist at all.

CHAPTER X.

LAST VISIT TO CHARLESTON — HER SON WILLIAM — REMOVAL NORTH OF THE OHIO RIVER.

Years came and went and Ann Bailey grew old. Long she had gone on foot from one extreme of the Valley to the other, stopping where she pleased and staying as long as she pleased; for she was welcome everywhere. From what can now be learned, it is believed that she made her last visit to Charleston in the summer of 1817.

The late venerable Laban Hill, of Mason County, who when a mere youth, accompanied his father, Jonathan Hill, to a pioneer home on Eighteen Mile Creek (now in Putnam County) in 1816, informed the writer some years ago, that in the spring of 1817, he went to spend the night at the house of Ira Dilno, a neighbor of his father, and that late in the evening, there arrived no less a distinguished personage than Ann Bailey, then in the 75th year of her age and *walking* to Charleston to visit friends. This statement is verified by that of Robert Warth, Esq., aged ninety-two years, of Ravenswood, West Virginia, who is still living and who says that he met her about six miles above Charleston, walking toward that place, in the summer of 1817.

No evidence of a later visit appears and it is presumed that in that year, she for the last time visited the associates of more eventful years. How long she remained we do not know, but Mr. Hill says he saw her in the *spring*. Mr. Warth says it was in the summer when he saw her near Charleston. She therefore probably spent several weeks or possibly months on and near the scenes of many of her adventures.

It is seventy-four years since Ann Bailey was on the streets of Charleston. What changes have taken place since that time! Then, clad in her border costume, she went from house to house and in all, the story of that perilous ride and a hundred other adventures was recited. A new generation had appeared and the rehearsals found listening ears. Imagine Ann Bailey passing along Capitol Street today. What a remarkable personage she would be! How strange would be the contrast where now move a cultured and refined people, enjoying every luxury which wealth can buy. But they would do honor to the memory of Ann Bailey.

It will be remembered that when Ann Bailey entered upon her career of adventure and daring, she left her fatherless son, William, then but seven years of age, under the protection of Mrs. Moses Mann, then of Augusta, but later of Bath County.

How long he remained at the Mann homestead we have no way of knowing. Whether he grew to manhood in Augusta or came with his mother and stepfather to the Kanawha Valley, cannot now be learned; but certain it is that soon after the erection of Cooper's blockhouse, on the Kanawha, he was there a frequent visitor. There he wooed and won the heart and hand of Mary Ann Cooper, who was the daughter of Leonard Cooper, who was as brave a man as ever found a home on the banks of the Kanawha. In the year 1800, William Trotter, then in the thirty-third year of his age, took his affianced in a canoe to Gallipolis where they became husband and wife, and a tradition states that they were the first Virginians married in the old French town.

William Trotter appears to have been a practical business man at the time of his marriage, and was possessed of some means. In 1814 he purchased, for the sum of twelve hundred and seventy-five dollars, a tract of two hundred and forty-six acres of land situated on the south side of the Kanawha about three miles from its mouth. This land was part of Washington's survey of ten thousand nine-hundred acres, which he surveyed for himself in October, 1770. Fielding

Lewis, of Hanover County, Virginia, as one of the Washington heirs, inherited thirteen hundred acres of this land; two hundred and forty-six acres of which passed into the possession of his son, Robert Lewis, the entire estate being divided among the heirs of Fielding Lewis; by survey made by Robert McKee, surveyor of Mason County, August 30, 1813. The portion of the land inherited by Robert Lewis was sold by Henry C. Dade, his attorney in fact, to William Trotter.

Here he built a house and continued to reside three years, his heroic mother making her home with him when he sold the land to William Sterrett, the consideration being fourteen hundred dollars, current money of Virginia. The deed of transfer bearing date March 18, 1817 may be seen in Deed Book D, page 229, in the Mason County Clerk's office.

Now, without a permanent home, he looked around and not finding a satisfactory purchase, he passed beyond the Ohio River and in the year 1818, in what is now Harrison Township, Gallia County, Ohio, bought two tracts of land; one of one hundred acres from Paul Fearing, and another of two hundred and sixty acres from Benjamin Joy. There he removed with his family the same year.

CHAPTER XI.

THE REMOVAL AND RESIDENCE NORTH OF THE OHIO RIVER — ANN BAILEY'S CABIN — HER DEATH AND BURIAL — HER DESCENDANTS.

Ann Bailey was bitterly opposed to the removal North of the Ohio River. Fifty-seven years she had spent in Virginia. Here were her friends and companions in war and in peace. Here slept all that was mortal of both her husbands, and now, at the age of seventy-six years, it seemed hard indeed — that she must be severed from the scenes of so many years to find a home among strangers. But the best interests of an only son were there, and with him she must go.

The home was selected in what was then the wilderness, back from the Ohio, about six miles from what is now Clipper Mills post office, Gallia County, Ohio. Here the son plead with the mother to stay with him, but she refused to do so. If she must be severed from her Virginia friends, she had others at Gallipolis and she would be near them.

She returned there, and on the hill just below the town and overlooking the Ohio River, she reared with her own hands a pen of fence-rails which she covered and thatched with straw, and in it attempted to live. An excellent view of it — together with the portrait of Ann Bailey — is shown in the frontispiece, which the author has permission to use through the kindness of Henry Howe, Esq., the venerable historian and the distinguished author of the *Historical Collections of Ohio*.

Here she remained but a short time for her son came and, with the aid of friends, induced her to accompany him to his home. There she consented to remain upon the condition that he would build, nearby his own, a cabin in which she should dwell alone. This he did and there she spent the remainder of her life.

For years she was a familiar character on the streets of Gallipolis where she was often a visitor. Usually she walked the entire distance of nine miles; but frequently, she came up in a canoe, which she could manage with the dexterity of an Indian.

On the streets she carried her rifle, and when interrogated as to the accuracy with which she could use it, would relate in the broadest English accent, how she once sat upon the back of her favorite horse Liverpool and shot "a howl on a helm tree across the mouth of the Helk River." With increasing age came many eccentricities, and she became known as "Mad Ann;" but none ever dared to so designate her in her presence. As long as she was able to visit Gallipolis, she found a welcome in the hospitable homes of the French settlers at that place. The her canoe often lay at rest beneath the willows on the Virginia shore, while she visited friends of the olden time on Mercer's Bottom.

But an eventful life was now near its close. Early Tuesday morning, November 22, 1825, she came from her own cabin to that of her son's, and informed her daughter-in-law that she was going to Gallipolis that day, and at the time complained of being ill. The daughter-in-law insisted that she should lie down, have some breakfast, and go to town on the morrow when she would feel better. She yielded and remained in bed until late in the evening, when she arose and persisted against persuasion in going to her own cabin; but she asked that two of her grandchildren — Phebe, aged eight, and Jane Anne, aged six — should accompany her. Certainly they were anxious to go with grandma, and after penning the ducks for the night, and filled with glee at the thought of staying all night with Grandma, ran along the path ahead of her and the trio reached the humble cabin. A fire was built and they — youth and old age — sat around it, the little ones listening in delight to the many stories related by Grandma, who loved to entertain the eager ears.

The shades of night gathered and darkness settled around that lonely cabin. There was but one bed; the cold, chilling winds of November blew fiercely outside, and the bed was taken from the stead, spread down before the fire and the three – the little one in the middle – nestled down for the night. The fire smouldered on the hearth and the light faded into darkness. All slept, but Phebe grew cold, and but half awake, called aloud to her grandmother, but no answer came. In her fright she called again, but all was still; then in her terror, she awoke the little one and told her that Grandma was dead. Without clothing and beneath the starlight, the little naked limbs, exposed to the wintry blast, and bare feet in the sparkling frost, they ran screaming toward home. Fond parents heard the wails of the little ones and hastened to meet them. They told the story of death, and Mr. Trotter, with some men who had been assisting him in gathering corn, hastened away; and entering the cabin, found that the soul had passed from earth and the great heart that had throbbed with patriotism and love for eighty-three years was stilled forever. Ann Bailey, the Heroine of the Great Kanawha Valley, had passed to eternal rest.*

Then there was a gathering of the settlers from all around, who came to perform the last sad rites of humanity. George Waugh, who lived hard by, made a rustic coffin; and without a funeral service, for no minister was near, all that was mortal of her who saved the garrison at Fort Lee, was laid to rest in what is still known as the Trotter Graveyard; and in an unmarked and almost nameless grave sleeps all that was earthly of Ann Bailey. England gave her birth; Virginia, a field for action; Ohio has her dust.

The birth or death of the great has given celebrity to spots of earth, and that in which Ann Bailey sleeps should not be forgotten.

---

*__Author's Note:__ The facts here, given relative to the death and burial were obtained from the aged Mrs. Phebe Willey, of Clipper Mills, Ohio, who was the elder of the grandchildren sleeping with Ann Bailey the night of her death.

As long as heroism is appreciated by a free people, that long should the memory of those who have given the best examples of it be cherished, and the grave of Ann Bailey should be marked by a shaft of enduring marble. But give the school children of Gallia County and the Kanawha Valley an opportunity, and they will erect it.

ANN BAILEY'S DESCENDANTS

William Trotter, as has been stated, removed to Gallia County, Ohio, March 22, 1818. There he became a large land owner, and was for many years one of the Justices of the Peace for that county. He died March 26, 1831, aged sixty-four years, and is buried on an eminence over looking the Ohio, three-fourths of a mile below Clipper Mills. His wife survived him more that forty years and is buried by his side.

They had issue:

1. **Philip**, born in 1801; married Hannah Codington, of Lawrence County, Ohio and became the father of three daughters and one son.

2. **Elizabeth**, born in 1803; married William C. Irion, and had issue, four sons and three daughters, one of the former dying in infancy.

3. **John**, born in 1805; in 1832 he rode to Gallipolis, left his horse hitched to a post and was never afterward heard of.

4. **William**, born in 1807; wedded Rosanna Houck, of Gallia County, and yet survives. They had issue, five daughters and three sons.

5. **Mary**, born February 11, 1811; wedded James Irion, and yet lives. She is the mother of six sons and six daughters.

6. **Davis**, born in 1813; wedded Sarah Knight, and had two sons. He died at Rockport, Indiana, several years ago.

7. **Sarah**, born in 1816; married John Gilmore, of Gallia

County, and became the mother of five sons and two daughters.

8. **Phebe**, born January 6, 1818; married Thomas Willey, in 1851, and had issue, four daughters, the youngest of whom married John Williams, present post-master at Clipper Mills. Phebe was the elder of the grand-children who were sleeping with Ann Bailey the night of her death.

9. **Jane Anne**, born 1820; married John S. Northup, of Gallia County, and became the mother of two sons and one daughter. She was the little one who slept in the middle on the night of death.

10. **Nancy**, born in 1822; wedded Francis Strait, of Gallia County, and had issue, six sons.

Thus it is seen that of Ann Bailey, there is a long line of descendants, now scattered over the West and South and numbering from two to three hundred. Wherever they have gone they give evidence of having inherited that endurance, physical strength and longevity, which distinguished her from whom they are descended. Brooks Irion, one of her great-grand-sons, in 1881, at Poughkeepsie, New York, ran five hundred miles against time, winning by two hours and eight minutes. The following year he went to Europe, and in Edinburgh, Scotland, ran a hundred mile race in which he broke the world's record by five hours and thirty-five minutes and was thus regarded as the swiftest man on foot then living. Returning home he engaged in the study of law and is now practicing in Kansas.

Of all her descendants but one, Simeon Irion, Esq., of Charleston, is now living in the Kanawha Valley.

FINIS.

PART II

ANN BAILEY

*Thrilling Adventures of the
Heroine of the Kanawha Valley*

**Truth Stranger than Fiction as Related
By Writers Who Knew the Story**

Mrs. Livia Simpson-Poffenbarger

Editor and Publisher of First Edition
Point Pleasant, West Virginia
1907

ANN BAILEY

VIRGIL A. LEWIS

So much interest was taken in the Ann Bailey articles that appeared recently that we have decided to publish the series of articles of this Heroine of the Kanawha Valley, who is buried in Tu-Endie-Wei Park on the East side, while the remains of her husband Richard Trotter are buried with the other dead of the Battle of Point Pleasant within the enclosure of the 40 foot square marked by the Col. Charles Lewis Chapter, D.A.R., with granite corner stones.

    Hon. V.A. Lewis, State Historian and Archivist, contributed the following to The State Gazette *in October, 1901 which we now reproduce, together with the story in prose by Mrs. Messinger and the poem by Mr. Robb.**

A ll that was earthly of Ann Bailey the Pioneer Heroine of the Great Kanawha Valley, that has not crumbled to dust, has been removed to Point Pleasant and re–interred in Tu-Endie-Wei Park. It is therefore now time to eliminate from the story of her wonderful career and life of adventure as scout and messenger everything of a mythical legendary, fabulous, and fanciful character, and to learn and to know the real narrative — the truth — regarding that record of female heroism which has no parallel in the annals of the Border Wars. The keeping of her grave is now in the care of the Col. Charles Lewis Chapter, Daughters of the American Revolution, and

---

*Publisher's Note: The poem appears in its entirety beginning on page 27 of Part I; published in the original 1891 book, it was reprinted in this booklet from 1907. It has not been duplicated in this 1998 edition.

they must answer a thousand questions regarding her whose bones they keep. Ann Bailey was herself a Daughter of the Revolution, a real one, who served her country faithfully and well when that struggle was in progress. The this western border was the "Back Door of the Revolution" and the men and women who kept back from it the savage allies of Great Britain were the "Rear Guard of the Revolution." Ann Bailey was one of these; and the school children should be able to tell to the thousands who will henceforth visit her tomb the real story of her life.

The following facts obtained from Border Annals, from official records, and from persons who knew Ann Bailey, will help them to do this:

1742 — Ann Bailey, whose maiden name was Hennis, was born in Liverpool, the western metropolis of England; the home of her father, who in early life had been wounded at the battle of Blenheim, while serving under the Duke of Marlborough. She was named for Queen Anne.

1747 — When five years of age her mother took her to London to visit relatives, and for the first time, and probably the last, she saw the splendors of the British capitol. While there she witnesses the execution, April 9th, of Lord Lovet on a charge of treason. (See any good history of England.)

1748 to 1760 — She resided in Liverpool and attended school in that city.

1761 — Both parents were dead and she was alone in a great city. This year she crossed the Atlantic to join her relatives, the Bells, who had emigrated to Virginia some years before. A journey over the Blue Ridge brought her to their home near Staunton in the Shenandoah Valley.

1765 — She wedded Richard Trotter, who had been at Braddock's Defeat and was prominent in Border Wars. Representatives of his family still reside in the Shenandoah Valley.

1774 — On the 10th day of October, her husband Richard Trotter was killed in the Battle of Point Pleasant.

1774 to 1785 — Eleven years of widowhood. When she heard of the death of her husband, a strange wild dream seemed to possess her and she vowed revenge on the Indian race. Having matured her plans, she submitted them to Mrs. Moses Mann, then residing in Augusta, but afterward in Bath County. She approved them and gave a home to the orphan son. It was now that Ann Bailey abandoned that home life that had once been so dear to her and entered upon that military career which has made her name famous for all time. Clad in the male costume of the Border, with rifle in hand, she attended the militia musters and urged men to go to war against the Indians in defense of hopeless women and children; or to enlist in the continental army and fight the Britons from sea. Then she became messenger and scout, going from one frontier post to another, thus continuing that career of female heroism which made her name a familiar one to the pioneers.

1785 — She was again united in marriage, this time to John Bailey, a distinguished border leader of Southwest Virginia. He had assisted in carrying Col. Charles Lewis off the field when fatally wounded at the Battle of Point Pleasant. Rev. John McCue was the officiating clergyman (see Marriage Record, No. 1, p. 7, in the County Clerk's office at Lewisburg, West Virginia.)

1788 — She went with her husband to Fort Lee, which was built by the Clendenins that year on the present site of the city of Charleston, the capital of West Virginia. The husband was a member of the Garrison and she served at messenger between Fort Lee and Fort Randolph at Point Pleasant.

1791 — She made her famous ride from Fort Lee to Fort Savannah at Lewisburg to secure a supply of powder for the Garrison of the former place when it was besieged by the Indians. Having obtained this, she returned and thus saved the Garrison and other inmates from death at savage hands. The distance between the two forts was more that a hundred miles, the whole of it was a wilderness road.

1800 — Her son William, grown to full manhood, took Mary Cooper, whose home was on the farm now owned by George Pullins, Esq. on the Kanawha River about nine miles above Point Pleasant, in a canoe, to Gallipolis where they were united in marriage, the first Virginians married in the old French town (see court records of Gallia County, Ohio.)

1802 — Her husband, John Bailey, died and was buried on the Joseph Carroll farm, fifteen miles above Charleston, on an eminence overlooking the beautiful Kanawha and there he now reposes. A second time Ann Bailey was a widow and she went to live with her son William Trotter. She rode back and forth from Point Pleasant to Lewisburg and Staunton, acting in the capacity of letter carrier and express messenger, and thus she was employed for several years.

1817 — She made her last visit to Charleston and there and in that vicinity spent the Summer of that year.

1818 — She removed with her son to Harrison Township, Gallia County, Ohio; he having sold his farm on the Kanawha (about three miles above Point Pleasant) the preceding year to William Sterrett, the consideration being fourteen hundred dollars, current money of Virginia (see records, Mason County Clerk's Office, Point Pleasant, West Virginia.)

1820 — About this time she was a frequent visitor at Gallipolis where she was ever a welcome visitor in the homes of the old French Settlers at the place. Her home was nine miles away and she was in the habit of walking the whole distance.

1825 — November 22nd — Ann Bailey died suddenly at night while sleeping with her two little grandchildren; one of whom, the aged Mrs. Willey, still lives at Gallipolis. For seventy-six years her remains reposed in the Trotter graveyard in the vicinity in which she lived, her grave being kept green by her descendants.

1901 — The members of the Point Pleasant Battle Monument Commission learned that the relatives of Ann Bailey were willing that her bones should be removed to Point Pleasant. On Saturday, October 5th, Hon. John P. Austin, accompanied by Mr. Norman Gibson, of Henderson, West Virginia, was dispatched to the graveyard in Gallia County, Ohio, where on that day the remains were exhumed and the next day conveyed to Point Pleasant; where, on the 10th of October they were re-interred in Tu-Endie-Wei Park under the auspices of the Col. Charles Lewis Chapter, Daughters of the American Revolution, and here they will repose, while thousands who hereafter visit the spot will inquire the story of her life.

ANN BAILEY

MRS. LILLIAN ROZELL MESSENGER

Why the history of this remarkable heroine, known and loved in the earliest colonial period, is not more extensively published and exploited in history and biography, along with others of the American Revolution, is not clear to the patriotic student. Especially when this woman's courage and bravery is of the same stuff and ranks with *Joan of Arc*, and the hero *Crockett* of the *Alamo* fame. Such bravery, like high mentality, is not confined alone to one sex. Ann Bailey's heroism was but an added proof of the fact that "Love (a portion of God) is the high-priestess of Truth;" and it, with mind, not necessarily depends upon educational processes — though, they both *innately demand* expression in the highest forms known.

The expression in deeds, of this heroic soul, began sometime before the Declaration of American Independence.

First, a few words about the country, the scene of her notable *warfare*, for so it was. Not many of us today have as yet even glimpses of the rich, historic, Revolutionary lore, embedded in the old Colonial States. The student is more familiar with the histories of Massachusetts, New York, the Carolinas and Virginia, from which West Virginia was ultimately formed. The history of the latter and the Kanawha Valley is of thrilling interest; its records forming links

between the early Indian wars, and the struggle for American Independence. *The whole success* of the *Colonists* in this great valley, the
Kanawha, proved to be of vital importance to the whole country.

Four miles west of Ronceverte and eight and one-half miles from
the Greenbrier, White Sulphur Springs, with Chesapeake and Ohio
Railroad, is the thriving colonial town of Lewisburg, West Virginia,
located in the midst of grand mountain scenery. Here still dwell many
scions and descendants of Revolutionary heroes and families, whose
warriors first conquered the wilderness and its savage foes, only to
turn their brave faces to fight the British armies, for our American
freedom.

Near this town of Lewisburg, in that early day of savagery, was
first *Fort Union* and also Fort Savannah, subsequently merged into
Lewisburg and named for the famous patriot Colonel Charles Lewis.
Farther down the Kanawha Valley, near the Ohio line, is the famous
place called Point Pleasant and where occurred one of the bloodiest
battles of the time that proved of far-reaching importance to the
colonies. This was the period of events, that brought forth the patriotic deeds of our Western Heroine, *Ann Bailey*. Point Pleasant dates
back to the arrival of Gen'l. Lewis' army in 1774. At this point once
stood old *Fort Randolph*; where now rest the remains of the brave
men who crossed wild rugged mountains through a savage wilderness
160 miles and fell in that bloody battle of October 10, 1774.

Now we'll digress here to add something of a more recent event,
namely: The Ladies Monumental Society, which was organized in
1860. The society was regularly chartered under the laws of the State
of Virginia and the fund with its accumulated interest amounted to
$2,000. The Civil War, disturbing conditions at Point Pleasant, the
society did not further push the work and by that time most of the
participants in that organization had passed to the other world. In
June of that year the Col. Charles Lewis Chapter, D.A.R., was organized and under their inspiration the historic spot was purchased at a
cost of $9,000 and by that society dedicated as a park, being given the
Indian name Tu-Endie-Wei. The ashes of the heroine Ann Bailey were
conveyed from Clipper Mills, Ohio, and entrusted to the "*Col.
Charles Lewis Chapter*," and here interred by the side of our soldiers

she had bravely risked her life to save, the event being the 127th anniversary of the battle of October 10, 1774.

And now we come to one of the greatest deeds of this heroine's life — scarcely equalled in any annals of warfare. Ann Bailey, born Ann Hennis, was a native of Liverpool, England. She was early left an orphan (her father one of Duke Marlborough's soldiers, lost his life in battle) and, at 19 years of age, she came to America to live with some old friends, the Bell family, at that time located in the wilds where now is the town of Staunton, Virginia. Here she married a brave young man, Richard Trotter, who was slain by the Indians. 'Twas at this juncture our heroine donned a semi-male attire made partly of buckskin used in those days and took the gun (perhaps her husband's), determined to protect herself and her little child and also avenge the husband's death.

Some years elapsed, filled with strife and bloody events, when the brave woman again wedded a soldier by the name of Robert Bailey. She went with him to old Fort Union, thence to Fort Lee, leaving her little son in care of protecting friends.

One hundred miles west of old Fort Union and Fort Savannah, was Fort Lee (now the site of Charleston) at the junction of the Kanawha and Elk. The fort was now threatened by a savage horde, hovering not many miles from the beleaguered garrison. Their powder was nearly exhausted, which created the wildest dismay among our men. Colonel George Clendenin called the garrison together to know who of the band would volunteer to risk their lives in an effort to save the garrison from slaughter. It meant the ride to, and return from, old Fort Union or Savannah (now Lewisburg), one hundred miles away. Brave men paled and looked at each other in dismay that appalled them. A dead silence fell. Only one voice was heard in a determined tone, and said: "*I will go.*" Every inmate of that beleaguered fort recognized the voice of *Ann Bailey*. None ever doubted her bravery, her integrity and patriotism. The fleetest horse of the stockade was brought. The heroine bade her husband a silent farewell. They all surely believed she could not fail, for did she not bear a charmed life? The gate was opened; horse and rider disappeared in the trackless forest. Onward, onward, day and night, sped the heroine

Ann Bailey, past Kanawha Falls; past Hawks Nest; up the silvery course of the New River, rushing like destiny, through realms of solitude, shade and darkness. Lastly, emerging a little out of the savage desolation, this brave woman beheld the Greenbrier mountains against the eastern sky, and saw the forest on the Lewisburg hills and the walls of Fort Savannah rose to view. She reached the Fort. Those inside recognized a familiar voice; the gates opened; a great welcome was given Ann Bailey. Very quickly she was telling the commandant the state of affairs at Fort Lee and their need and her mission. The delay was short. She was furnished with an additional horse, and both were laden with powder. The officer in command offered to send a guard with her, but she declined; riding one horse and leading the other, she began her perilous return. Night and day she pressed on; and at last, nearly exhausted but animated by hope of saving the garrison, she reached Fort Lee amid shouts, the echoes of which died among the wild hills around; she was ushered within the gates, having accomplished the most daring feat recorded in the annals of the West. The savages still hovered near; but the next morning the garrison marched forth, and after a spirited action, forced them to raise the siege, and thus that feeble garrison, on the site where a capital city now stands, was saved from butchery by this heroism. This memorable event occurred when the heroine was in her 49th year. In addition, the latter part of her long, lonely perilous journey was under a savage fire. Though the wild red men had a legend (so often she escaped their bullets), that she was protected by the Great Spirit, terming her the "*Great White Squaw*," many times refusing thereafter to fire on her in her flight.

The faithful horse she rode on this famous journey was presented to her by the soldiers of Fort Lee. She named him "Liverpool" in memory of her native place. It is recorded that more than once the faithful animal saved her life.

This heroine lived a number of years after peace and independence was declared; making her home with her only son, married and located near Clipper Mills, Gallia County, Ohio. She was fond of her two grandchildren; and to the last she retained her exceptional devotion to nature and primitive forms of life in country and forest.

Her death was sudden and painless. The last summons came at midnight, while the two little children rested by her side.

In her case, we can but recall the following lines as expressive of the passing of this great heroic soul:

" The gray days close behind her; and
　　time's a wind that blows
Among her little snow-rimmed hills and
　　scant trees ashed with snows;
Her spinning wheel sings to the blaze of
　　vanished bloom and blade:
Her books are folden at old tales and
　　rhymes that dead men made.

Let all her years go softly, and the quiet of
　　the stars
Is shed across her pallid couch between
　　her window-bars;
And death shall find her wise with prayer;
　　and death shall be no more
Than a friend who rideth late at night
　　and knocks upon the door!"

PART III

AFTERWORD

MAP & PHOTOGRAPHS

INDEX

ABOUT THE AUTHOR

ACKNOWLEDGMENTS & NOTES

AFTERWORD

This small gem of a book came to my attention while researching another text about the Battle of Point Pleasant. It had been hidden away at the bottom of a shelf in the non-circulating stacks of the Mason County Library.

The legend of Ann Bailey is a familiar one to residents of Point Pleasant, but the details have been obscured by the march of time. This text takes care of filling in the blanks.

The booklet of *Thrilling Adventures* presented itself to me in a most unusual way: by error. At the West Virginia State Archives, that book was retrieved in place of *Life and Times*, and I realized that it *had* to be included with the earlier book.

After much discussion with a handful of associates in the publishing field, it was advised that the book *not* be altered for political correctness, but rather, presented as an historical text. Interpretation can then be up to the reader. It is readily apparent how our societal attitudes have changed over a century with regards to ethnicity and gender.

Of greater importance is the retelling of Ann Bailey's story. Having driven U.S. Route 60, the Midland Trail of her famous ride, I am in awe of her riding that same route on horseback in the dark under duress (not that it isn't stressful today). Also, the territory she

regularly covered in her later years showed her amazing stamina; some
people seem destined to living larger than life. And Mr. Lewis, by
interviewing people who actually conversed with Ann Bailey, was able
to chronicle for all of us the details of that life, and the underlying
character of the woman who lived it.

It is my hope that you have enjoyed this book. I consider it a
fortunate find to be able to reintroduce it to a new generation, and
that by doing so, hope that Mr. Lewis himself would be pleased.

Mark S. Phillips
Publisher
September 30, 1998

MAP SHOWING ANN BAILEY'S TIMELINE

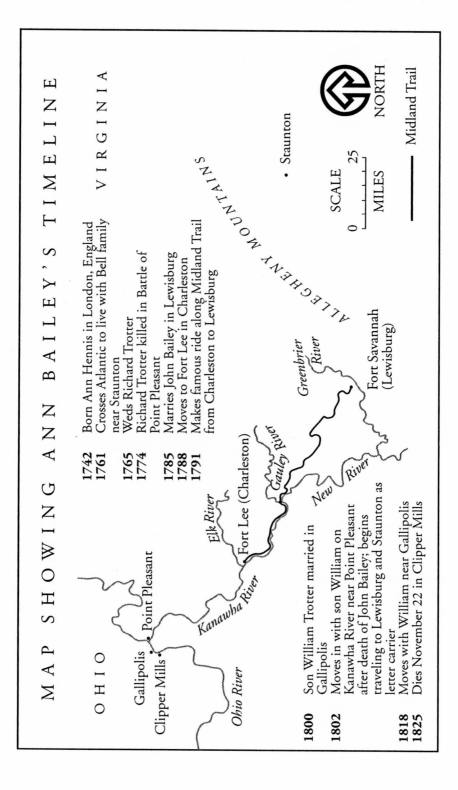

OHIO

VIRGINIA

Ohio River

Clipper Mills

Gallipolis • Point Pleasant

Kanawha River

Elk River

Fort Lee (Charleston)

Gauley River

New River

Greenbrier River

Fort Savannah
(Lewisburg)

ALLEGHENY MOUNTAINS

• Staunton

NORTH

SCALE
0   25
MILES

———— Midland Trail

1742 Born Ann Hennis in London, England
1761 Crosses Atlantic to live with Bell family near Staunton
1765 Weds Richard Trotter
1774 Richard Trotter killed in Battle of Point Pleasant
1785 Marries John Bailey in Lewisburg
1788 Moves to Fort Lee in Charleston
1791 Makes famous ride along Midland Trail from Charleston to Lewisburg

1800 Son William Trotter married in Gallipolis
1802 Moves in with son William on Kanawha River near Point Pleasant after death of John Bailey; begins traveling to Lewisburg and Staunton as letter carrier
1818 Moves with William near Gallipolis
1825 Dies November 22 in Clipper Mills

Tu-Endie-Wei State Park at the confluence of the Ohio and Kanawha Rivers, Point Pleasant, West Virginia. Scene of the battle of October 10, 1774, where Richard Trotter, Ann Bailey's first husband, died in combat. Both Trotter and Bailey are interred in the park in separate graves.

Monument to the magazine (storage bunker) where the ranking officers and gentlemen were buried. It is not known if Richard Trotter was buried here or in a common grave. Though he was a seasoned veteran, he held the rank of private. *Tu-Endie-Wei State Park, Point Pleasant, West Virginia*

Ann Bailey's remains were moved from Ohio to this grave in 1906. The grave marker was fashioned from lightning-damaged stone removed from the park's obelisk. *Tu-Endie-Wei State Park, Point Pleasant, West Virginia*

Inside the Mansion House of Tu-Endie-Wei State Park hangs a shadow box with interesting contents: a length of Ann Bailey's hair has been ornamentally braided as a remembrance.

The home of Virgil Lewis, Brown Street, Mason, West Virginia. Listed on the National Register of Historic Places in 1979, it serves today as a museum and the meeting place of the Mason City Historical Society.

West Virginia Historical Marker, Mason, West Virginia.

INDEX

of *Life and Times of Ann Bailey*

Adams, Alvin 48
Alexander, Col. John 42
Alexandria 11, 44
Allegheny Mountains 14, 18-20, 40, 45, 49
American Revolution 17, 18, 38, 41, 42
Ann Bailey's Cave 46
Anne, Queen 5, 7, 12
Arbuckle, Capt. William 38, 39
Arbuckle, Mathew 39
Augusta County 9, 10, 13-16, 21, 52
Averill, Mr. 9
backwoodsmen 13, 17
Bailey, James 18
Bailey, John 7, 19, 22, 36
Balcony Falls 38
Ball, James 38
Barkley, John 36
Barlow, Joel 43
Bath County 52
Battle of Blenheim 5
Battle of Culloden 6
Battle of Point Pleasant 15, 37, 38, 41
Bell Creek 36
Bell family 9, 10
Belleville 24
Bennett, Dr. Jesse 42, 43
Big Sandy River 19
Blue Creek 36
Blue Ridge 10, 14
Boone, Daniel 23, 38-41, 43

Botetourt 42
Braddock, Gen. Edward 11
Braddock's Field 11
Brownsville 44
Bryan, Andrew 37
Buell, William P. 7, 9
Buffalo 39, 43
Bullitt, Col. Thomas 21
Bullitt, Cuthbert [father] 21
Bullitt, Cuthbert [son] 21, 22
Burden's Grant 21
Burgess, Edward 19
Camp Lookout 27
Camp Union 15, 38
Campbell's Creek 36
Capitol Street 52
Carroll, Joseph farm 36
Catawba Settlement 19
Charles Town 22
Charleston 22, 25, 36-38, 43, 45, 46, 48, 51, 52, 59
Charleston Height 27
Clarke, Col. G. R. 39
Clendenin [ranger] 20
Clendenin family 21
Clendenin, Alexander 22, 37
Clendenin, Archibald 21
Clendenin, Charles 21
Clendenin, Col. George 21-23, 26, 37, 38, 40
Clendenin, Ellen Mary 22
Clendenin, Parthena 37
Clendenin, Rebecca 49

Clendenin, Robert 22
Clendenin, William 21, 37, 38, 48, 49
Clendenin's Fort 22
Clermont [Oh.] *Courier* 27
Clipper Mills 55, 57-59
Cobb, Fleming 43
Codington, Hannah 58
Colonial Army 14
Cooper, Leonard 23, 41, 42, 52
Cooper, Leonard [son] 42
Cooper's blockhouse 42, 52
Cornstalk, Chief 14, 39
Cremeans, Reuben 43
Crockett, John 19
Cross Lane[s] 27
Cumberland City 11, 19
Cunningham [ranger] 19
Dade, Henry C. 53
Deborah 1
Dickinson [ranger] 19
Dilno, Ira 43, 51
Dinwiddie, Gov. 21
Donnally, Andrew 20
Donnally, Andrew 43
Donnally, Catherine 43
Dounie 6
Dunlop [ranger] 20
Dunmore County 43
Dunmore, Lord 14, 39
Dunmore's War 14, 39, 40
Edinburgh 59
Eighteen Mile Creek 38, 51
Elk River 15, 18, 22, 23, 29
Eulin, Benjamin 38

Ewing, Gen. Thomas 37
Fairfax County 42
Farnesworth, Ephraim 48
Fearing, Paul 53
Forbes, Dr. D.C. 46
Fort Charleston 24, 25, 29, 35
Fort Clendenin 7
Fort Cumberland 11
Fort Duquesne 11
Fort Edward 18
Fort Fincastle 18
Fort Henry 27
Fort Lee 22, 25-27, 35, 38, 45, 57
Fort Loudoun 18
Fort Randolph 18, 22, 38, 39
Fort Savannah 18, 26, 34, 39
44th Royal Infantry Regiment 11
48th Royal Infantry Regiment 11
France 2, 6
Frankfort 40
French 500 44
French Revolution 43
Gallia County 49, 53, 55, 58, 59
Gallipolis 43, 44, 47, 52, 56, 58
Gauley Bridge 27, 35
Gauley River 18, 26, 28, 34
George, James 43
Gibb's Trace 38
Gibbs, Luman 38
Gilmore, John 58
Gordon, [Mr.] 11
Goshorn, John H. 3
"Great Spirit" 46
Greenbrier County 14, 20, 35, 43, 48
Greenbrier Mountain 26
Greenbrier River 22
Greenbrier Valley 48
Greenlee, Maurice 43
Hamilton family 20
Hannan, Esom 43
Hannan, Thomas 43
Hanover County 53

Hanover Presbytery 20
Hansford, John 43
Harnden, William 48
Harriman, Shadrach 43
Harrison Township 53
Harrison, Joseph 43
Havre de Grace 44
Hawk's Nest 26, 34
Hawkins, William 43
Hereford, Capt. John 42
Hereford, William P. 43
Hill, Johnathan 43, 51
Hill, Laban 51
Hinton, Mary 42
Hogg, Peter 43
Hogg-Bennett, Elizabeth 43
Holley, Bailey 43
Holloway, James H. 47
Holloway, Joseph H. 42
Hostein River 19
Houck, Rosanna 58
Howe, Henry Esq. 55
Huddlestons, Paddy 43
Illinois 39
Indiana 39
Irion, Brooks 59
Irion, James 58
Irion, Simeon Esq. 59
Irion, William C. 58
Irions, Mary 3, 49
Isabella 2
Israel 1
Jackson's River 18
James River 9, 10, 38
James, King 6
Joy, Benjamin 53
Kanawha County 23, 36, 40
Kanawha County 43
Kanawha Falls 26, 28
Kanawha River 15, 22-26, 29, 32, 35, 36, 38, 39, 42, 46-48, 52
Kanawha Valley 10, 19, 20, 23, 24, 27, 38-41, 43, 46-48, 51, 52, 57-59
Kanawha Volunteers 43
Kansas 59
Kelly's Creek 24, 36
Kenton, Simon 38
Kentucky 23, 39, 40

Knight, Sarah 58
la Belle Riviere 44
Lavalette 2
Lawrence County 58
Lee, Gov. Henry 22, 23
Leon 43, 45
Letart Falls 38
Lewis [ranger] 19
Lewis, Fielding 52, 53
Lewis, Gen. Andrew 38, 41
Lewis, John 10
Lewis, Robert 53
Lewis, Thomas 22
Lewisburg 7, 15, 18-20, 26, 34, 35, 39, 45, 47
Liverpool (city) 5-7, 10, 11
Liverpool (horse) 35, 45, 56
Loch Moras 7
London 6, 8
Lovat, Lord 6-8
Mackley, Jacob 43
"Mad Ann" (nickname) 56
Madison, James 39
Mann, Mrs. Moses 17, 52
Marietta 37
Marlborough, Duke of 5
Martin, James 19
Maryland 41
Mason County 40, 42, 43, 47, 49, 53
Mason County Riflemen 43
Maumee 43
Maxwell, John 19
McClenachan [ranger] 19
McClenahan, Capt. Robert 39
McClenahan, Catherine 39
McClenahan, Jane 39
McClung family 20
McCoy, Theophilus 43
McCue, Rev. John 20
McCulloch, Mary 3, 37, 48
McKee, Robert 43, 53
McMullin, Joseph 39
McNeale, Geneive 37
Meigs, R.J. [father] 37
Meigs, R.J. [son] 37
Menager, Edward S. 43
Mercer's Bottom 38, 42, 43, 48, 56
Moffett 20

Monongahela River 11
Morris, Henry 43
Morris, John 23
Morris, John 43
Morris, Leonard 43
Morris, William 43
Mount Tompkins 34
Mountain Cove 27, 34
Mud Lick Creek 41
Muddy Creek 14, 21
Nelson, James 43
New Hampshire 38
New River 26
Northup, John S. 59
Northwest Territory 44
Ohio 57
Ohio River 14, 15, 18, 25, 38, 40, 43, 44, 53, 55
Ohio Valley 15
Paris 43
Pennsylvania 43
phantom rider 46
Philadelphia 43
Pickaway Plains 39
Pioneers of Greenbrier 20
Point Pleasant 15, 16, 18, 19, 22-24, 37-43, 45-47
Potomac River 11, 18
Poughkeepsie 59
Powell, Thomas 43
Preston [ranger] 19
Prince William County 21
Pruit, Robert 43
Pullins, George W. Esq. 42
Putnam County 51
Randolph, Gov. 23
Rangers 19
Ravenswood 51
Red House 27
Renick family 20
Reynolds, John 38, 43
Richwood 22
Ringsbury, James 43
Roanoke River 18
Roanoke Settlement 19
Robison, Isaac 38
Rockbridge County
Rockport 58
Rue Neuve, des Petits Champs 43, 44
Ruffner, David 43

Ruffner, Joseph 43
Ruffner, Tobias 43
Scarey (Scary) Creek 28, 41
Schuykill 40
Scioto Land Company 43
Scotland 6
Scott, Thomas 43
See, Michael 38
See, Michael 43
Sewell Ridge 27, 34
Shawnee warriors 46
Shenandoah River 48
Shenandoah Valley 10, 48
Six Mile Island 43
Slack, John Sr. 3
Smith, Samuel 43
Spain 1
Springhill 43
Staunton 10, 12, 18, 41, 45, 47
Steenbergen, John W. 42
Sterrett, William 53
Stewart, Capt. 39
Stewart, John 20
Strait, Francis 59
Stuart, Capt. John 35, 39
Tackett, Lewis 43
Teays, Thomas 41, 42
Thirteen Mile Creek 40, 41, 46
Timber Ridge Church 20
Treaty of Greenville 37
Trotter graveyard 57
Trotter, Davis 58
Trotter, Elizabeth 58
Trotter, Jane Anne 56, 59
Trotter, John 58
Trotter, Mary 58
Trotter, Nancy 59
Trotter, Philip 58
Trotter-Willey, Phebe 3, 56, 57, 59
Trotter, Richard 7, 9, 11-16
Trotter, Sarah 58
Trotter, William (son) 14, 52, 58
Trotter, William (grandson) 58
Turley, John 41, 42
Tyler, Isaac 38
Upper Tennessee River 19

Valley Department 23
VanBibber, Capt. Jesse 39-41
VanBibber, John 38
VanBibber, Mathias 38, 43
VanBibber, Rhoda 40
Versailles 6
Virginia 9, 10, 12-14, 18, 21, 38, 40, 42, 43, 55, 57
Virginia Provincials 11
Waggener, Col. Charles B. 3
Wallace, Andrew 43
Warm Spring Mountain 18
Warner, Boudridge 43
Warth, Robert Esq. 51, 52
Washington City 37
Washington, George 11, 14, 52, 53
Waugh, George 57
West Virginia 20, 22
WV Historical and Antiquarian Society x, 41
West, Col. George 42
"White Squaw of the Kanawha" 46, 47
Willey, Thomas 59
Williams, John 59
Williamsburg 14
Wilson, John 43
Winchester 18, 44
Winfield 46
Withers, George 43
Witten, James 19
Wynn, Oliver 19
Yorktown 42
Young, Jacob 43
Zane, Elizabeth 27

ABOUT THE AUTHOR

Virgil A. Lewis (1848–1912) was a native of Mason County, West Virginia. Born in a log cabin, Lewis was nine when his father died, leaving him to assist in the upbringing of his younger siblings. As he grew older, he held various jobs including grocery boy, shipping clerk, drug assistant, and printer's devil.

Fascinated by history, he received a teaching certificate; his career path led from educator to principal, superintendent, editor, author, State Superintendent of Schools, and the first State Historian of West Virginia.

As an author, he had thirteen works published, the most notable of which was *History and Government of West Virginia* in 1896. It was utilized as a state textbook for over fifty years.

He and his wife Elizabeth were the parents of six children.[4]

ACKNOWLEDGMENTS

The assistance of many individuals contributed to the republishing of this text: Greg Carroll and Bob Taylor of the West Virginia State Archives; Duryea Kemp and Lisa Wood of the Ohio Historical Society; Lois Test and Mildred Gibbs of the Mason City Historical Society; Alice Sauer of the Col. Charles Lewis Chapter, D.A.R.; Janet Reed of the Mason City Library; Bill and Cheryl Clements of Quarrier Press of Charleston; Patrick Grace, Ph.D., of Publishers Place, Inc. of Huntington; and to my children, Ellie and Ethan, many thanks for their support.

All photos by the publisher. Image of the author courtesy of Mason City Historical Society.

NOTES

1. Fry, Plantagenet Somerset: *The Kings and Queens of England and Scotland,* 1990 (Grove Weidenfeld, New York) 165.

2. Rice, Otis K.: *A History of Greenbrier County,* 1986 (Greenbrier Historical Society, Lewisburg, West Virginia) 27-28.

3. *A Walking Tour of the Historic City of Gallipolis, Ohio,* brochure published by The Ohio Valley Visitors Center of Gallipolis.

4. *History of Mason County, West Virginia,* Lewis, Virginia E.: "The Family of Virgil A. Lewis" 1987 (Walsworth Publishing Co., Inc., Salem, West Virginia) 198-199

Printed in the United States
30985LVS00003B/103-243